TO MY FATHER, WITH LOVE

First published in the United States in 2000 by
Periplus Editions (HK) Ltd., with editorial offices at
153 Milk Street, Boston, Massachusetts 02109 and
5 Little Road #08-01, Singapore 536983.

Design and special photography copyright © 2000
Carlton Books Limited, London
Text copyright © 2000 Alice Whately

Library of Congress Card Number: 00-105782

ISBN: 962 593 942 3

North America
Tuttle Publishing
Distribution Center
Airport Industrial Park
364 Innovation Drive
North Clarendon, VT 05759-9436
Tel: (802) 773-8930
Tel: (800) 526-2778

Japan
Tuttle Publishing
RK Building, 2nd Floor
2-13-10 Shimo-Meguro, Meguro-Ku
Tokyo 153 0064
Tel: (03) 5437-0171
Fax: (03) 5437-0755

Asia Pacific
Berkeley Books Pte Ltd
5 Little Road #08-01
Singapore 536983
Tel: (65) 280-1330
Fax: (65) 280-6290

First edition
06 05 04 03 02 01 00   10 9 8 7 6 5 4 3 2 1

Editorial Manager: Venetia Penfold
Senior Art Editor: Barbara Zuñiga
Designer: Smith
Project Editor: Zia Mattocks
Picture Researcher: Catherine Costelloe
Special Photography: Graham Atkins-Hughes
Production Manager: Garry Lewis

Printed and bound in Dubai

contemporary
eastern

interiors from the orient

Alice Whately

PERIPLUS

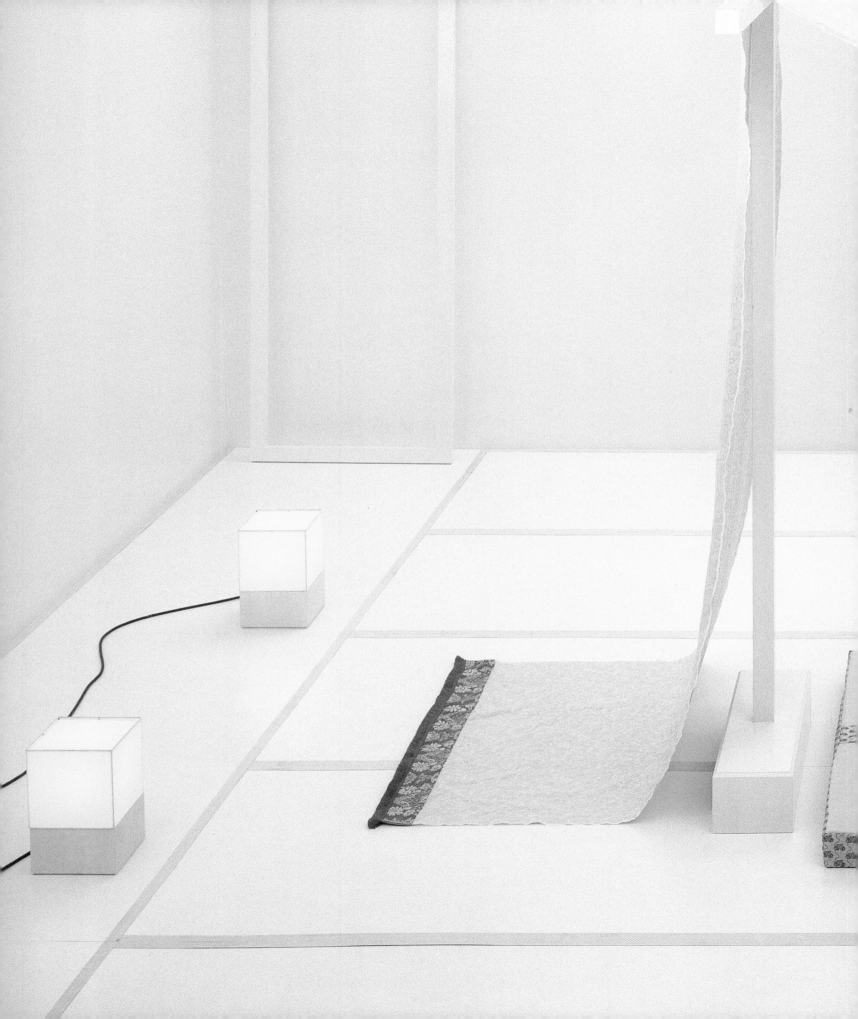

contents

Introduction

The Western fascination for all things Oriental is not a new one. Since medieval times when travellers returned from the Far East, overwhelmed by the colours, furnishings, and artefacts there, Orientalia has remained a permanent feature in Western furnishings.

In the eighteenth century, the demand for eastern exotica reached its height. Vast shipments of silks, damasks and toile de Jouy were imported, along with ornate furniture, delicate porcelain and crates of tea. Being rich enough to buy these opulent goodies was another thing entirely; those who could afford to set a cluster of Ming vases against a backdrop of hand-painted wallpaper did so in order to show off the size of their purses.

These days, our yearning for the Orient has a more spiritual bent. In a bid to supersede the sour taste of over-consumerism, we have turned to the ancient philosophies of the Far East in search of inspiration. As a result, Buddhist retreats are replacing beach holidays; tai chi has become the new PE and feng shui is practised in supermarkets, airports and banks. Our homes are changing, too. The desire to create a peaceful haven in which to retreat from the frantic pace of twenty-first century life has resulted in fluid, natural interiors – with open-plan spaces taking over from small, cluttered rooms and organic furniture replacing self-conscious designs in synthetic materials.

The first signs of change came in the mid-1980s when shops, hotels, clubs and bars metamorphosed from noisy, cluttered spaces into serene, white cubes, scented with incense and paved with soft stone. 'Less is More' became the new catchphrase, and the concept of minimalism (adopted from the purist principles of Zen Buddhism), started to attract an increasing number of homeowners tired of living with a plethora of possessions.

As a result, colour is slowly being dispensed with, and furnishings are kept to a minimum. In addition, the contemporary Eastern spin on paring down sees streamlined cupboards instead of bulky dressers and crisp white cubes in place of cushion-strewn sofas. This influence is also having a squeaky-clean effect on Western bathrooms. Taking our cue from the Japanese, who view bathing as essential to spiritual well-being, contemporary Eastern bathrooms feature a shower (for getting clean), a bath (for meditative wallowing), and precious little else; lotions and potions are stashed from view, and accessories come in natural materials such as stone and wood.

In tandem with the fashion for living spaces that are free from visual distractions comes the desire to reconnect with nature. Once again, contemporary Eastern homes look towards the Orient, taking inspiration from the architectural styles of Japan, Thailand and Indonesia. As a result, we are eschewing outside walls in favour of Japanese-style sliding glass doors (for a barely-there divide between outside and in), and knocking through inside walls in a bid to create the light, airy interiors witnessed in Thailand and Indonesia. This design ethos goes hand-in-hand with the trend for natural furnishings; these days we want our coffee tables to be hewn from organic hunks of wood, our cushions to be trimmed with shells and our homes to tinkle with the sound of running water.

Having created a haven of peace and tranquility – be it a spare white cube or a nature-lover's lair, it is only understandable that we should want to fill it with calming sounds, soothing smells and beautiful ornaments. Once again, Oriental disciplines set the pace, inspiring a multitude of spiritual accessories including candles, incense, wind chimes and crystals. Meditative practices are also catching on in the West: taking our cue from Zen Buddhism, where the art of contemplation has been practised for hundreds of years, the contemporary Eastern home emphasizes the importance of a shrine, aquarium or moon-viewing pavilion in order to help Westerners focus and calm the mind.

The contemporary Eastern look is not all holier than thou, however. Fans of colour, clutter and clashing patterns can furnish their homes with modern exotic styles, which include opulent opium dens, boho chic and kingdoms of kitsch. A delight for maximalists the world over, the rich palette, intricate embroidery, ambient lighting and quirky irreverence of Eastern-style furnishings offer a variety of different styles for the contemporary Eastern home.

In this book I have chosen to focus on China, Japan, Thailand, Indonesia and Vietnam as the countries best-suited to illustrating the Eastern design styles that can be reinterpreted for a contemporary look. Using the gem-bright palette of China as a starting point for Eastern interiors based on modern exotica, I then turned to the contrasting beauty of austere Japanese-style interiors, which offered endless inspiration for the clean, minimalist looks featured in Born again Zen. The plethora of natural materials and breezy, open-plan influences of housing in Thailand and Indonesia provided the fodder for Outside In, while the brilliant lacquerware, religious observances and craftware witnessed in Vietnam inspired Living in Harmony.

1 Every movement of human life is affected by form and colour

BEN NICHOLSON

In direct contrast to the fashion for neutral interiors, the new exotica is rich, lush and opulent. Taking its inspiration from the decadent opium dens of 1930s Shanghai, in addition to sybaritic silks from Vietnam, Thailand and Indonesia, contemporary Eastern furnishings mix colour with texture and mysticism with modernity.

Since the days of the Roman Empire when the first Eastern imports arrived via the Silk Road, Orientalia has fascinated Westerners. Fabrics, fragrances, gemstones, lacquerware and spices redolent of exotic lands were sold in trunkloads by merchants plying their trade to Europe via central Asia. As a result, Eastern exotica has been a staple in Western homes for centuries – slipping in and out of fashion, but never disappearing completely, thanks, in part, to the advent of chinoiserie – the European take on Eastern style.

Modern Exotic

Currently at the forefront of fashionable home furnishings, the modern exotic look is rich and dramatic: colours clash with unashamed ebullience, wallpaper is busy and brash, and lacquerware gleams with brilliant reflection. That said, contemporary Orientalia also offers plenty of scope for subtlety, with elegantly proportioned furniture, fine porcelain, intricate woodcarving and delicate embroidery. The current trend for dark wood continues – with low benches and boxy chairs carved out of wenge, palmwood and ziricote – while red and yellow are clear winners in the colour stakes, followed by black, purple and flashes of metallica.

The next four sections of this chapter cover the key looks of modern exotica: Pagoda Pads concentrates on colours, patterns and furnishing styles which combine age-old Orientalism with contemporary influences; Opium Dens recalls the decadence of 1930s Shanghai – when Nirvana was reached by smoking a pipe rather than chanting a mantra; Mai Tai showcases the sybaritic silks of Thailand and the legacy of Jim Thompson; and Eastern Eclectic concentrates on super-decorative styles, including Boho Chic and Oriental Kitsch.

Pagoda Pads

Left **The graceful pagoda image in fashion designer Matthew Williamson's boudoir helps to balance the horizontal lines of the wicker chest.**
Right **Offering instant glamour, a swathe of scarlet will pump up your interiors in a flash.**

Pagodas

Although they were originally introduced from India along with Buddhism, pagodas are integral to images of the Far East. Built to protect saintly relics, or to house religious documents commemorating important events, their ornate and majestic appearance has evolved over the centuries to incorporate traditional Chinese architectural styles.

Most of the pagodas in the Far East are found in China and Vietnam. In Vietnam pagodas are a focus of social, political and religious life, while the temples that have been restored following the Cultural Revolution in China seem sadly incongruous, with their photo booths, concession stands and gift shops evoking few of the traditional beliefs which underpinned the country's civilization for 3,000 years.

For Westerners the pagoda is a blatant symbol of Eastern exotica: its traditional, curved lines (thought by the Chinese to bring good luck), graceful symmetry and colourful, glazed roof tiles are mystical and alluring, inspiring the citation of harmonious contemporary furnishings with a similarly exotic feel. As a result, the pagoda-pad look includes rich fabrics, elegantly proportioned furniture and slashes of brilliant colour, including imperial yellow, green and red.

Seeing Red

Seductive, sensual and sexy, red will pump up your interior in a flash. Offering instant glamour, a swathe of scarlet is perfect for anyone longing to break free from the confines of cream – but be warned – a little goes a long way.

Renowned in China as the colour of happiness, red is viewed by Westerners with a kind of peaky

Red has always been the centre. It is the way we view the interior

ANISH KAPOOR, SCULPTOR

mistrust. According to decorating magazines, painting your bedroom crimson is a major health hazard, causing stress, insomnia, or worse still, dreams filled with bloodthirsty images. Living rooms, kitchens and bathrooms fare little better; scarlet shrinks room proportions, say the experts, and causes tempers to flare.

Whether you choose to believe any of the above is up to you. Without a doubt, full-on red is not for the faint-hearted. However, there are numerous shades of this fabulously rich hue – from cherry to cinnabar and burnt umber to brick – which will guarantee a vibrant colour injection without necessarily causing divorce.

Compromise is one answer. Eastern exotica is easily attained with dashes of brilliance rather than blocks of colour: teaming red with neutrals creates a cracking combination, while ceramic

Vietnamese stools in shiny scarlet look brilliant against a backdrop of matt black. Similarly, red and gold also work well together – and is a combination which fashion designer Matthew Williamson used in his intimate, womb-like boudoir. Cashing in on Eastern sensibilities, where red and gold are *de rigueur*, Williamson's glinty flashes give the room the appearance of a fabulously upmarket bordello.

Traditionally a religious combination, red and gold have been the signature palette of China since the Han Dynasty. Yellow represents heavenly glory, red means vitality and life – and a combination of the two pervades Chinese furnishings – from red dowry chests fastened with circular brass clasps to yellow silk tassels hanging from poppy-coloured lanterns, and golden dragons running riot over scarlet silk.

Above left **Full-on red is not for nervy insomniacs. Choose your shade with care and you can create an atmosphere that manages to be both seductive and relaxing.**
Right **Scarlet and black is a striking and dramatic colour combination. Team it with splashes of yellow, white and indigo for a striking result.**

Modern Metallica

In the West, the Chinese love of gold and the Thai love of silver is a look that's fast catching on as an exotic complement to vivid Eastern colours. In particular, the mercurial charms of modern metallics are catching our attention. Gold, silver, copper and bronze offer a palette of shimmery sheens on fabrics, paints and wallpapers. There are myriad ways of introducing metallics into your home: go for gold – *à la* Grand Palace in Bangkok, or opt for flashes of iridescence.

Racier than rugs, metallic floor tiles are available in a variety of rich finishes. Brushed silver aluminium tiles look great in kitchens and bathrooms (with coordinating silver grout sealer), while ceramic tiles in copper, bronze and pewter are perfect for halls and passageways.

Alternatively, you could paint your walls in silver or gold. Aluminium emulsion reflects and absorbs light, as well as changing colour as it catches different lights during the day. For a less shiny effect, distressed metallic paints look carelessly expensive, while sheets of mirrorflex mosaic tiles (think disco-kitsch) in bronze and silver open up dingy spaces. Gold or silver leaf

Left **Mini mirrored wall tiles offer a contemporary twist to the Eastern love of gold and silver, bronze and brass.**
Clockwise from right **Classic bowl shapes go glam with modern metallica, and a smart silver trim luxes-up workaday chopsticks.**

applied to cupboards and door panels is gorgeously decadent; gold-painted beading gives walls modern definition and even fibreboard, varnished in golden honey tones looks expensively exotic.

As a look, the use of brilliant reflectives is easily consolidated: polished chrome door knobs, gilded mirrors, silver floor cubes and bronze bowls all add a steely glint, while satin sheets and cushions provide a softer, more slippery sheen. As far as ornaments go, a bowl of silver lacquered pebbles, a golden Buddha, or a gilded incense holder are ideal for putting on the glitz.

Pagoda Pads

Chinoiserie

Chinese style, or chinoiserie as it later became known, was a dominant force in Western decoration throughout the seventeenth and eighteenth centuries. Blending exotic Eastern influences with European style, chinoiserie remains one of the most consistent strains in Western taste today – although it should be remembered that the furniture and furnishings originally produced were largely a product of the European imagination, as opposed to a true representation of Chinese style.

Chinese Chippendale is a case in point. Using Oriental fretwork in addition to simple lines (also inspired by Eastern designs), the resulting spindly-legged tables, and chairs with ornamental backs, were not representative of anything found in Eastern homes. (Similarly, wallpaper made by the Chinese was designed specifically for flamboyant Western tastes.) The taste for chinoiserie has endured throughout the twentieth and twenty-first centuries: from Art Nouveau to the Modern Movement, artists, potters, textile manufacturers and furniture designers have all raided chinoiserie's rich repository of colours, techniques and motifs.

Japonism – a popular supersedent to chinoiserie in the late-nineteenth century – presents a similar story. More recently referred to as Japonaise, this take on rigorous Japanese style included softer-edged bamboo furniture, and images of geisha girls simpering on fans. The sparseness of Japanese design, popular in Europe and the USA, spawned a fashion for simple lines which remains a dominant influence in furniture design today.

Above **Gilded Oriental fretwork lends a graceful edge to this Chinese Chippendale chair, with its typical high back and sides.**
Left **The spare aesthetic of Japanese furniture design has appealed to Western purists since its introduction in the late-nineteenth century.**

Right **Golden glints add a touch of class to milliner Philip Treacy's eclectic interior. In his sitting room, Treacy confidently mixes a graphic modern rug, sculptural chair and a traditional daybed draped with a kitsch chinoiserie throw, featuring gaudy flowers, fluorescent fish and golden threads.**

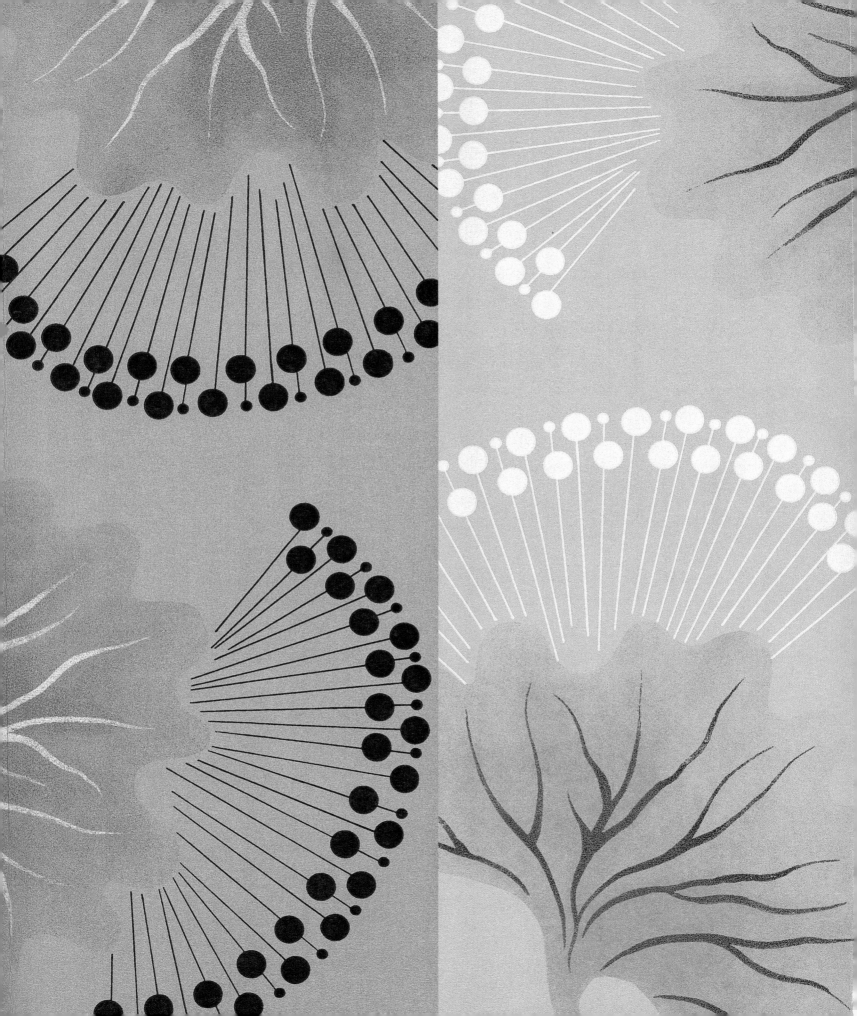

Left **Pucci-esque florals with an Eastern spin, by British designer Neisha Crossland.** Below **Charming Chinese motifs are still popular on Western walls.**

Pagoda Pads

Hailed as a key design feature for modern interiors, chinoiserie-style wallpaper has undergone a makeover. Since its introduction to Western homes in the early eighteenth century, when papers were imported from the Far East as separate sheets rather than rolls, Europeans have loved the asymmetric, Oriental designs, which were jazzed up with glitzy metal highlights. Popular motifs have included round-faced Chinamen fishing, flying kites or drinking tea in pavilions flanked by weeping willow trees.

To this day, many antique patterns are still available. Others serve as inspiration for contemporary designs, and Japanese 'leather papers' are also enjoying a revival. Popular in the 1880s, these heavily-embossed lacquered wall-hangings enjoyed a renaissance in the 1960s, when they were machine produced, and are increasingly sought after to this day.

Rather than appear centre stage, however, modern wallpapers are content to wait in the wings, with one wall of Eastern motifs contrasting with three walls of complementary paint colours or no-nonsense neutrals. This restrained approach offers an appealing compromise, especially for those with minimalist leanings. And with a plethora of gorgeous papers on the market, including hand-blocked motifs in aluminium leaf, Eastern-inspired florals or hammered copper bronze reminiscent of Issey Miyake pleats, the choice is endlessly exotic.

Opium Dens

Thou hast the keys of Paradise, oh just, subtle, and mighty opium!

THOMAS DE QUINCEY

Left **Contemporary modern meets vintage hotpotch: Verner Panton's purple plastic backdrop complements a range of bedlinen made from patches of antique silk kimonos.**
Right **The pleasures of the pipe: opium-smokers lie back in a dreamy stupor.**

Opium-smoking has been synonymous with China for years. In Chinese literature, references to opium date back to AD 220, and by the time the Arab opium trade was established in the seventh century AD, China was already originating a home-grown product. This is an important point to remember in the light of the accusation that it was eighteenth-century European traders who introduced trafficking – although they were guilty of corrupting China to an unforgivable degree with what was called 'foreign mud'.

The vision of the opium den as a secret hideout, swathed in sumptuous brocades and rich velvets, was upheld by non-smokers, whose feverish imaginations conjured up glamorous images of decadence and depravity. Certainly, opium dens were finished with daybeds and soft pillows, but they were far from glamorous. Instead, addicts lay in a befuddled stupor or writhed in the grip of horrible hallucinations. Even so, opium dens have managed to retain their mystical allure, prompting an exotic decorating style based on indulgent hedonism. Excess is vital, with lots of louche, loungy furniture, velvet lighting, sybaritic fabrics and dark decadent colours.

There is a black which is old and a black which is fresh
HOKUSAI

Right and far right Black is back. Layer ebony, jet and liquorice for a blinds-down, lights-out look – or pump up the pace with a smattering of furnishings and accessories in jewel-bright shades.

Black

For a blinds-down, lights-out kind of look, black is the ideal medium, offering a decorating style that is intimate, seductive and chic. But although black is currently being hailed as the 'colour' of the moment, exploring your darker side requires courage and commitment. As a result, it's important that you decide just how far you want to go before plunging into the abyss.

The advantages of black in interior decoration are numerous. As a base colour it provides a fabulously blank canvas for a wide variety of different looks: combine it with purple for a mystical feel, with red for a seductive aura, with gold for gilty decadence, or with white for monochrome chic. Nor do you need to stick with complementary colours; a black backdrop offers liberating design choices in terms of palette, furnishings and ornamentation, but try not to overdose – a few key pieces in black, offset with brilliant flashes of colour – present the most dramatic results. Black is also great for layering. With around 50 variations to choose from – including ebony, charcoal, liquorice and jet – there's plenty of scope for shady options.

Left **Presenting a modern spin on the traditional Japanese interior, this bedroom balances the sharp angles of the parquet floor with soft circles in the form of disc-shaped tatami mats, spherical lighting and decorative boxes.**

Pattern and Texture

Lots of action and distraction is another option for black interiors, especially when it comes to flooring. The contemporary fashion for rugs (hailed as the new rock'n'roll in home furnishings) offers an ideal choice for brooding spaces, providing focus and weight. A time-honoured favourite in Eastern homes, from the dark-bordered tatami mats patronized by the Japanese to the intricately woven rugs beloved by the Chinese, contemporary rug designs include stark, abstract patterns with a minimum of three colours. The preferred shape is circular, and materials range from long-haired goat to cropped cashmere, although for opium-den chic a shaggy, luxuriant pile is best. Alternative options for floors include black parquet, black rubber tiles or dark tarmac studded with pebbles. For unalloyed opulence, however, lacquered floors in lustrous liquorice win the day.

Black is also a great way to display a range of interesting textural contrasts: decorate black plywood walls (lightly stained so that the grain still shows through) with pictures framed in jet lacquer, or fling a charcoal satin throw across the back of an inky leather sofa. Sumptuous black brocades look great mixed with tough-looking industrial furniture, while decorative Indonesian daybeds complement dark Chinese silk, resulting in a look that manages to be both intimate and chic at the same time.

Opposite **Creating a room-within-a-room is a particularly Eastern sensibility. Folding screens have long-since provided the fastest, and easiest, way to section off space.**
Left **Combining a love of glossy dark wood with clean straight lines, Chinese furniture is designed around simple squares and elegant rectangles – with chairs, armoires, wedding chests, lights and side tables all demonstrating a beautiful symmetry.**
Below **Even garden furniture takes a boxy stance, as seen in these rustic chairs, which blend into the leafy environs even though their design is a basically formal one.**

Darkwood Furniture

More than any other decorative art, Chinese hardwood furniture embodies the restrained beauty and elegance of the East, with a satisfying blend of harmonious lines and understated details. Viewing straight lines as more restful than curved ones, the Chinese have always loved square, boxy styles – with chairs, wedding chests, wardrobes and neck pillows all designed to the basic shape of cubes and rectangles. Carved teak furniture is typically Chinese, as is the use of darker hardwoods such as ebony and wenge,

a look that continues to be the number-one choice in contemporary decorating circles.

The modern spin on Chinese cuboid furniture has been a consistent feature in home furnishings over the past 60 years. Following in the minimalist footsteps of late American architect and designer Donald Judd, designers such as Christian Liaigre and Spencer Fung continue to produce sexy square pieces, with sofas, tables, lamps and footstools all reflecting the tranquility of Oriental furniture. There's no doubt about it, it's hip to be square.

Lacquerware

The most tactile of all Oriental finishes, lacquerware is made by highly-skilled artists across the Far East. The process is a lengthy one, with layer after layer of resin (made from the sap of the Chinese lac tree) applied to hardwood or bamboo. Fashioned into furniture or decorative containers, the resin is then painted, using soot- or vinegar-soaked iron filings to turn it black, and cinnabar to produce a rusty red colour. Styles are either plain, or decorated with a gold, silver or tortoiseshell inlay. In Thailand, lacquerware is often set with mother-of-pearl, providing intricate decoration for furniture, musical instruments and statuary.

Contemporary lacquerware offers a glossy furnishing alternative to traditional, matt styles. Available in brilliant colours including emerald green, canary yellow, orange and red, its expensively indulgent sheen lifts interiors in an instant. Black lacquer is the most exotic of all: choose an inky nest of side tables or a black lacquered screen for a broodingly sophisticated look, and accessorize with Eastern-inspired furnishings such as a cool set of matt black ceramics, or a black Moor fish swimming in a bowl filled with dark gravel.

Mai Tai

Since the days of the Roman Empire, Westerners have been fascinated by silk. Originally used to create elegant sheath dresses, the slippery fabric has long been a staple in home furnishings, with cushion covers (left) **remaining a perennial favourite.** Above right **Fashion designer Betsey Johnson's New York home is awash with shimmery fabrics.**

The Story of Silk

Before the discovery of the sea passage to India, the Silk Road was the most important connection between East and West. In AD 200 this transcontinental route served as the main conduit of commerce, linking the Roman Empire in the West with the imperial court of China. Along with gems, tea and spices, silk was a major export, although the route was not given its romantic moniker until the 1880s.

Roman women, in particular, were fascinated by silk – demanding an increasing supply of the fabric that made such flattering robes. Not surprisingly, canny merchants kept the manufacturing process a closely-guarded secret, and with death sentences hanging over anyone who spilled the beans, China managed to maintain its monopoly on silk until about 200 BC, when the secret of its manufacture became known in Japan and Korea. In the West, the knowledge was acquired in the sixth century AD, when silk-worm eggs were eventually smuggled through. By the thirteenth century, Chinese silk was used for European church vestements, and by the nineteenth, Canton was exporting large numbers of silks depicting Eastern motifs such as dragons, phoenixes and flowers.

Traditional Motifs

The Chinese are a deeply superstitious race, relying on a number of auspicious symbols to bring good luck. These motifs permeate Chinese life and thought, with pine trees, cranes and clouds representing long life and many sons, and fish symbolizing abundance and wealth. Peace is represented by vases; beauty and dignity by peacocks and pheasants; and connubial bliss by mandarin ducks. The seasons are also shown symbolically, with a combination of bamboo, pine and plum blossom for winter, iris or magnolia flowers for spring, peony or lotus for summer and chrysanthemums for autumn.

The most dominant motif is undoubtedly the dragon. Viewed by the Chinese as a friendly creature, which reigns supreme over all animals, the dragon came to be identified with the Emperor during the Han Dynasty, and is thought to symbolize the yang (male) energy. It is often depicted alongside the phoenix, which represents the yin (female) force, associated with the Empress. Imperial, five-clawed dragons are also greatly revered in Vietnam, where they symbolize mastery over land and water, and hence the King himself.

Contemporary Chinese silk continues to feature auspicious motifs, while the fashion for chinoiserie on skirts, shoes and handbags has reached its gilded arms into home furnishings. As a result, plush eiderdowns made from Cambodian wedding silk jostle with sheets sewn with tiny plum blossoms, and taffeta wallpaper complements patchwork floor cushions made from swatches of antique silk. Damasks have always been used in opulent decorating schemes, while formal Chinese robes or Japanese kimonos are still popular as Western wall-hangings.

Less intricate than Chinese embroidery, Japanese silks maintain a sense of balance and space: typical designs include trelliswork and tartan, while a more subdued palette contrasts with the gem-bright colours of Chinese silks. Recurring Japanese motifs include the pairing of plum blossom with pine trees, reeds with grasses and irises with wisteria, and are also deeply symbolic. The fleeting beauty of cherry blossoms represents the frailty of life, and the camelia, which flowers throughout the winter and then falls from the shrub, betokens the true qualities of the Samurai warrior, ever ready to die.

Top left **To this day Chinese silk is embellished with auspicious motifs. The mythological phoenix represents the yin force that is associated with the Empress.**
Left **The dragon is viewed as the Eastern equivalent of a guardian angel.**
Right **Motifs representing the natural world contrast with a black and white photo on a modern bag.**

Toile de Jouy

Originally serving as an expensive wall covering, toile de Jouy was used as a hard furnishing fabric once the eighteenth-century demand for less expensive (i.e. paper) wallcoverings was met. Like Indian chintz, which was printed on calico, toile de Jouy is a decorative cotton fabric, originally manufactured in China using engraved copperplates. Pleasure-loving Europeans (especially the French and English), loved the intricate ebullience of toile de Jouy, which adhered to a strict colour code of dusty rose, indigo or sepia on a white background. The designs were also safely familiar, depicting repeating patterns such as a mandarin descending a steep stairway, a brace of pavilions set in an airy landscape and fragile pagodas flanked by curving trees. Over the years, however, the patterns have evolved – with French pastoral scenes replacing many of the original Oriental ones.

Toile de Jouy has never really gone out of fashion. Still frequently featured in contemporary interiors magazines, the romantic blend of Oriental-style patterning and crisp French chic gives a clean, cottagey feel that is endlessly appealing. Modern designers either team it with plain blue or pink linens, or go for total coverage with surprisingly successful results. Combined with white, toile de Jouy on curtains, chair covers and beds looks fresh and coherent, rather than hectic and overdone.

Thai Silk

Although villagers in the north-east of Thailand have been weaving silk for centuries, it wasn't until after the end of the Second World War, following the destruction of leading silk industries in China, Japan, Italy and France, that Thailand, whose silk was noted for its thickness and sheen, emerged as a primary source. Credit is given to Jim Thompson, an American expatriate, for improving the looms, introducing long-lasting chemical dyes and taking samples of shimmering Thai silk to New York. The cloth he introduced to the USA was used to make the costumes for a new Broadway musical, *The King and I*. Shortly afterwards, *Vogue* magazine championed the sumptuous new silks, and within a short time increasing demand resulted in the creation of a world market.

Today, most of Thailand's raw silk is still produced on farms in the north-east of the country – and manufactured by a number of companies there. In addition, Jim Thompson stores around the globe keep the flag of Thai silk flying, selling bolt upon bolt of striped, checked and plain silks in muted shades – from no-nonsense neutrals to candy pinks, peppermint greens and bon-bon bright orange and yellow.

Above **American expatriate Jim Thompson kitted out his Bangkok house in traditional Thai style with low-level tables, elaborate woodcarvings and local artefacts.**
Left **Modern designers mix toile de Jouy with plain colours and simple furniture for a crisp contemporary style with a hint of exotica.**

Tea is more than an idealization of the form of drinking; it is a religion of the art of life

OKAKURA KAKUZO

Tea Ceremonies

The sound of trickling water,
The simmering of the kettle,
The simplicity and orderliness
The touch of the bowl and
The bitter flavour ...
And you thought tea
Was just something you had a cup of

ELLE DECORATION, 1998

The History of Tea

Tea is said to have been discovered by the Emperor Shen Nung in 2737 BC. Its popularity grew rapidly during the fourth and fifth centuries AD. During the Tang Dynasty (AD 618–906), the preparation and service of tea became an elaborate ceremony, while essential oils of jasmine, lotus and chrysanthemum flowers were added in the Song period for a subtler flavour.

The first seeds of green tea came from China to Japan in about AD 803. In the early twelfth century, a Japanese monk re-visited China and returned with a fresh batch of tea seeds, as well as an understanding of the teachings of the Rinzai Zen Buddhist sect. Tea-drinking developed alongside Buddhism, and whereas Chinese tea-drinking rituals have all but disappeared, the Japanese still practise a complicated and unique ceremony today.

Japanese Tea Rituals

The tea ceremony captures the essentials of Japanese philosophy and artistic beauty. Practised in a plain, thatched hut, simply furnished with an arrangement of flowers or single painting, the ritual aims to create a quiet interlude in which host and guests strive for spiritual enlightenment and harmony with the universe. Utensils are unpretentious, and when guests arrive they are greeted by the singing of the kettle (pieces of iron are arranged inside it to create sounds to suggest a far-off waterfall or wind blowing through pine trees). Elaborate rules dictate the way tea is whisked and served, and how utensils should be passed and admired.

Tea Today

Tipped to be the new urban trend, with Oriental tea houses taking over from coffee bars on every street, the demand for tea is growing steadily, especially in the USA. Sales of light, flavoursome assam tea from Indonesia match those of herbal varieties – rose- and cherry-scented sencha from Japan and magnolia, jasmine, chrysanthemum and orchid flavoured

Take your cue from the Japanese, who still practise lengthy tea-drinking rituals, and reward yourself with a long cup of refreshing afternoon tea (left). Although tea is still sipped from delicate bowls in the Far East (right), teaware in the West evolved to include handles and saucers (below).

teas from China. Japanese green tea is also popular: said to strengthen the heart, aid digestion and reduce the risk of cancer, its health-giving properties are attracting Westerners in their droves.

Modern Teaware

In the earliest Chinese records of tea-drinking, leaves were boiled in open pans. By the Ming Dynasty, the fashion for steeping processed leaves in hot water required a covered vessel in which to infuse the leaves and keep the water hot. Gradually, teapots evolved and when the Dutch began importing tea from China to Europe in the late sixteenth century, the stone teapots they used had wide spouts and broad bases.

The first tea bowls arrived in Europe in the mid-seventeenth century. Tiny and handleless, they increased in size over the next 100 years, when the addition of saucers (originally made in China and copied in Europe) was also witnessed. By the nineteenth century, full tea services were developed as the European taste for afternoon tea grew. Tea was also popular in the USA at this time, with New Yorkers following a tea-drinking etiquette similar to their European counterparts.

Contemporary Japanese teapots – in either delicate or sturdy shapes – are made from cast-iron with a glazed interior. Patterns include gentle water designs or a traditional spiked Eastern surface with matching trivets (bases). Used as aesthetic display items, along with stone Raku teacups, teak scoops and waxed bone teaspoons, traditional Japanese tea bowls are modelled on lotus flowers, fruits and bamboo trunks. Modern designs, however, tend to be stark and white with more decorative styles favouring green or a reddish brown colour, embellished with a simple pattern of spots or plum blossoms. In this way, Japanese artists allow the beauty of the stone to speak for itself.

Traditional Chinese teaware consists of the 'gugwan' (or covered-up) bowl, saucer and lid, which was designed in 1350, as well as fine, translucent porcelain decorated with the classic Willow pattern. The modern spin on porcelain tends towards the minimalist. Contemporary ceramics include elegantly simple teasets in timeless white, or cups, saucers and teapots dipped in celadon glazes for a slinky finish that makes them almost too beautiful to use.

Eastern Eclectic

More is More

In direct contrast to the Zen dictum 'less is more', maximalism celebrates flashy, trashy clutter, clashing colours, patterns and furniture styles. This look is perfect for hoarders who want to display their possessions, as well as fans of kitsch.

The key to this style is more complicated than it appears. Combining antique and modern furniture with bright colours and vigorous patterns, the thrown-together look is rarely an act of spontaneity. And while the high priests of Zen may view such apparently careless disarray as nothing more than a hotchpotch of sleazy souvenirs, clutter-mongers – such as fashion designer Betsey Johnson – know that eclectic style requires confidence, vision and flair.

'Everything I love is on display,' says Johnson, whose sassy New York home is filled with her possessions, all of which relate to different parts of her life. 'My home is an accumulation of my favourite junk,' says Johnson, who refuses to deny her existence by hiding her personal effects behind closed doors.

The effect of Johnson's home is one of ordered chaos. Flowered Versace rugs lie next to decorative Oriental ones, and jellybean-filled Buddhas jostle with embroidered Japanese fans. In the kitchen, glamorous gold and chinoiserie furnishings sit beside an industrial 1920s stove, while a medley of colour and pattern runs riot throughout the apartment – from yellow walls

Right and far right **Fashion designer Betsey Johnson's home is crammed with her cherished possessions.**

CHINESE
PAPER-CUTS

Jade Jagger
con le figlie Assisi e Amber

and lavender floors to chairs and cushion covers festooned with frowzy rose prints.

Having lots of stuff also creates a process of continual re-evaluation: 'You stop seeing what you have if you don't rearrange and start over again,' says Johnson, who constantly shuffles things around, and becomes instantly upset if anything goes awry in her 'careless' arrangements.

Matthew Williamson's London apartment is in a similar state of flux. Continually painting walls and moving the furniture around, the fashion designer's current obsession with the Far East is reflected in the images on his pinboard, where Oriental influences mix and match with Occidental ones, such as a black and white photograph of his muse, Jade Jagger.

Liking clutter is not symptomatic of a serious character flaw. Just as minimalists shudder at the concept of overkill, so maximalists become distressed at the thought of stashing their beloved possessions behind closed doors. Less is more only if you can cope with the idea of paring down. If you can't, keeping your environment clutter-free will prove a constant struggle, causing far more headaches than a room brimming with ephemera.

46   Right **Mix and match
diverse furnishings
and accessories for
true bohemian style.**

Boho Chic

It's an inescapable fact that global-style interiors take time to evolve. Genuine boho chic requires years of dedication as furniture and fabrics, trinkets and talismans must either be collected on trips overseas, or sourced at numerous flea markets and antique fairs. Exotic furnishings are far removed from the clean, minimalist lines of the modern home. Instead, boho chic takes its inspiration from cultures across South East Asia, where Chinese painting tables, Japanese wall-hangings, Thai silver, Vietnamese lacquerware and Indonesian ikat jostle with I Ching coins, gilded birdcages, bronze gongs and sandalwood fans.

Offering a classic example of ethnic eclecticism, Bonnie Young's house is a model of itinerant inspiration. As director of global sourcing for Donna Karan's Home Collection, Young is privy to some of the world's best artefacts – although the prevailing theme in her Greenwich Village townhouse is an Asian one.

'I try to make what I find abroad fit into the everyday lifestyles of European countries,' says Young, whose home features a silk robe from the Xishuangbanna region of China, a darkwood divan from Bali, glass beads from Indonesia and an antique wedding chest, which is hidden under the bathroom sink and used for toiletries. Huge, double doors leading into the main living area lend an airy Asian feel, while bolts of ethnic fabrics – from Indian paisleys to Vietnamese silk – add a softer edge, underpinned by a palette of cinnabar, saffron, black, bronze and nutmeg. These dusky colours are the signature shades of boho chic and help to create a warm Eastern coherence, as well as reduce the impact of Young's hard-edged furniture.

Decorated along equally eclectic lines, John Malkovich's guest bedroom at his home in Los Angeles blends Pacific Rim exoticism with a touch of old colonial. The bright, bohemian effect illustrates an arty idiosyncrasy which

Above **A Balinese divan in dark wood creates an effective focal point at the end of this long room.**

requires total style confidence. Mixing Oriental influences with Occidental ones, Malkovich teams silk Chinese textiles with gingham checks, and Chinese window panels with a picture of a Christian icon. Similarly, he diffuses the room's sultry feel with clashing textures and contrasting woods: a rough cotton rug lies next to the slippery silk of the quasi-Chinese bedcover, while the heavy Indonesian bed base, which has

been elaborately carved with elephants, contrasts with the delicate bamboo frontage of the floor-to-ceiling cupboards.

Producing a coherent style by clashing patterns, colours and textures is a case of trial and error. Taking your time is the number-one rule, and while boho chic is not ideal for those with an impatient streak, ethnic details, plus a few simple guidelines, will help to establish

Below **John Malkovich's
guest bedroom blends
Pacific Rim exoticism with
a dash of old Colonial.**

a base while you accumulate your global
furnishings. 'Distressing' is key to achieving
bohemian chic: beaten-up leather, chipped
paint, scarred wood and mottled mirrors are
ideal for setting the scene, as is lots of faded
colour (the bleached-out look is essential for
authenticity). Metallics should be burnished
(anything you can see your reflection in is
a definite no-no), and natural materials
are vital: stone, tin, bone, shell, raw silk
and muslin all fit the bill.

As far as details go, glazed Chinese roof
tiles in red or yellow introduce Orientalia into
kitchens and bathrooms, while chunky candles
add instant karma. Big ethnic beads, hammered
silver jewellery, chunks of crystal, handwoven
baskets and anything a bit 'off-centre' (i.e. not
machine-made) are all guaranteed to hit the
mark. Even minor additions such as a frondy
plant in a bronze container, a haphazard pile
of travel books or a potted orchid are a step
in the right direction.

Oriental Kitsch

Choose any number of fashionably iconic knick-knacks and you can be guaranteed they will have been made in the Far East. Thanks to manufacturers in China, Japan, Korea and Taiwan, Oriental kitsch is now a permanent feature in Western interiors – with pagoda-patterned bead curtains, cushions depicting Mao Zedong and Golden Rooster alarm clocks littering sofas, shelves and side tables. Introduce kitsch with a touch of sensitivity, however, and the result does not have to be trite: a serious side table dotted with a collection of Eastern curios can elevate an ordinary interior into an ironic one with a single playful flick. Similarly, an all-white bathroom decorated with a row of same-style snow domes looks voguey rather than vulgar.

But while a dash of kitsch is often all that's required, some people like to take 'bad taste' to the max, mixing beading, fringing, tassels and toys with gaudy colours, prints and chintz. Dangle-jangle is the order of the day, with rainbow-coloured wind chimes, cushions fringed with bells and musical cigarette-lighters all clamouring for attention against a backdrop of paper lanterns with neon-bright shades.

As far as Marie-Anne Oudejans is concerned, Oriental kitsch is about spiking corners of her home with lush pleasure zones. A fashion designer for her own label, Tocca, Oudejans's SoHo studio in New York is as unique as her clothes, with loud pockets of colour leading to quiet corners of calm. The ceilings are dotted with a variety of brightly coloured Chinese

Below left and below

Religious icons have always been a favourite with manufacturers of modern kitsch.

lanterns, the floors layered with exotic rugs and the walls covered with a chaotic collection of images. 'I've always liked building fantasy shrines,' says Oudejans, who draws inspiration for her fashion collections by linking disparate pictures, ornaments and memorabilia.

Best known for her girlie dresses, it's hardly surprising that silk is a dominant feature in Oudejans's apartment: 'The fabrics I use for clothes are also perfect for the home,' says the designer, who has also launched a soft-furnishings collection which includes a tactile range of silk sheets and pillowcases. Dyed in pink, lavender, lemon and lime, and embroidered with tiny plum blossoms, Tocca cushions, covers and throws are coveted by über models and lesser mortals alike.

Above right and above

For true throwaway chic, the rules are simple: the cruder and more garish the better.

We all need a splash of bad taste DIANA VREELAND

Opposite **Kitsch couture: gold lamé glams up this workaday sofa, while a cluster of red lanterns clashes courageously with a purple parasol and maribou-feather fan.**
Left and far left **The light from Chinese lanterns offers instant exotica at the flick of a switch. Or, glue a tea-light to the lantern's base – but don't leave it unattended.**
Below **Illuminate a favourite object or icon by adorning it with a necklace of fairy lights.**

Exotic Lighting

Ambient lighting is key to the spirit of the Orient, offering instant exotica at the flick of a switch. First off the blocks are coloured lights with variable settings to match your mood – as seen in hip hotels such as St Martin's Lane in London. Even better, at Ian Schrager's New York hotel, the Henry Hudson, guests enter the lobby illuminated by an intense 'halo' of neon light. More traditional, but equally evocative, Chinese lanterns come in pink, yellow and green, and are the ideal way to brighten up dingy corners, hallways and passages. Alternatively, a clutch of scarlet shades will pump up the pace in an instant, as well as cast atmospheric shadows.

Another option is to string a line of cube-shaped paper lanterns around your living space for a nice, even light. Fairy lights should be arranged in an artful pile or erected around the walls to produce linear pinpricks of luminosity. Glittery disco balls will appeal to fans of retro kitsch, while coloured-glass chandeliers are once again fashionable, offering the perfect choice for advocates of Eastern eclecticism.

2 In the beginner's mind there are many possibilities, but in the expert's mind there are few SHUNRYU SUZUKI

Purity, harmony, simplicity, serenity, peace. These words describe the ancient philosophy of Zen, which offers a calming antidote to the frantic pace of modern life. In terms of interior design, Zen is about paring down: materialism is replaced with minimalism, chaos with calm, and stress with serenity.

'The chance to retreat to an oasis of tranquility following a long day at the office is an enticing concept,' says architect John Pawson who, together with fellow Zen masters Claudio Silverstrin, Christian Liaigre and Anouska Hempel, spearheaded the 'Less is More' campaign in the mid-1980s, producing serene white spaces washed with diffused light. Bathrooms, designed along Japanese lines, were simple wooden affairs, furniture was built into the fabric of the house and ornaments were selected for their functionability as well as their aesthetic appeal. Not surprisingly, it wasn't long before the monastic look became the new religion for homeowners, who found the concept of living in a series of spare white cubes hugely appealing.

Born again Zen

Commonly viewed as a Japanese concept, Zen is actually an ancient Chinese belief which originated in the sixth century as a merging of Indian Buddhism and Chinese Taoism. This joining of the speculative with the practical, and the metaphysical with the earthy, was a bid to find the path to true enlightenment. In 1190 AD, Zen Buddhism was enthusiastically adopted by the Japanese and over the centuries the philosophy evolved to include three main design principles – simplicity, functionalism and minimalism – factors which have been reinterpreted by Western designers and architects since the nineteenth century.

The first Zen teachers came to America around 1905 and in the 1950s Zen Buddhism became cool, thanks to writers like Jack Kerouac, founder of the Beat generation. But it is the Japanese who continue to embrace the philosophy of Zen, refining small-space living to a fine art. In addition, Japanese architects, such as Tadao Ando, take inspiration from their own culture. 'Instead of simply pursuing superficial comforts, I re-examine what has been discarded in the process of economic growth and seek after only those things that are essential to human dwelling,' he says. 'With thought and restraint, it is entirely possible to create interiors that are ordered, sensual and relaxing, even if they are small.'

The typical Japanese interior is calm, understated and devoid of the myriad possessions that frequently fill Western interiors. Instead, Japanese homes recall the peacefulness of the past, paradoxically making them the modern classics that they are today.

The sections in this chapter cover the key areas of Zen living, including the power of paring down, the importance of space and light, Japanese-style bathing and the concept of streamlined storage.

Pure Style

Right **For an ordered sense of calm, combine natural materials with a few key accessories.**

Capsule Apartments

These days everyone is pushed for time, so a low-maintenance home is essential if you want at least one part of your life to run smoothly. Prune your possessions until you are left only with the things you need, and allow your home to evolve into a calming retreat from the outside world, a place where you can think clearly and act efficiently. Simplicity in interior style does not necessarily mean throwing out your most treasured possessions, however. Instead, simply store the things you don't use every day and follow the advice of William Morris, who urged his fellow Arts and Crafts designers to 'have nothing in your house that you do not know to be useful, or believe to be beautiful.'

In addition, it is possible to pare down in stages, replacing your shagpile with seagrass or your velvet drapes with simple Venetian slats. A sense of calm and order is easily achieved through the use of natural materials and carefully chosen furniture, but if the concept of minimalism still leaves you cold (yet you yearn for a quiet retreat when the going gets tough), keep one room clear to serve as an oasis of calm – rather than stripping out the entire house.

In Zen philosophy the presence of an equal number of natural elements is a central belief. This is mirrored in interior design, where serenity, simplicity and balance is wrought by elements of earth and water, fire and forest – components which can be introduced through colour as well as objects. For example, if it is not possible for you to introduce a water feature into your home, use an indigo cushion or a turquoise vase instead. Similarly, fire is mimicked by a candle or orange lantern, earth by small, rounded pebbles or a wooden floor, and forest by natural materials such as bamboo and teak.

Our life is frittered away by detail ... Simplify, simplify

THOREAU

Born again Zen

Conserving the mores of the past is an essential part of modern Japanese life. Ancient rituals such as taking your shoes off before walking into someone's house remain a national practice, while tatami mats – an age-old staple in Japanese interiors – continue as the number-one floor covering.

The tatami mat is literally interwoven into the fabric of Japanese life: people eat, sleep and die on these foldaway floor coverings, while advertisements in the windows of real estate agencies describe available spaces in terms of tatami-mat capacity. Measuring 1 x 1.8 m (3 x 6 ft), 'two tatami-mat rooms' in space-crushed cities like Tokyo and Kyoto are much more common than 20 tatami-mat rooms.

Tatami is made from woven rushes and has a reassuringly tactile feel. Contemporary alternatives with similarly springy qualities include golden-coloured coir, jute, seagrass, sisal, or wafer-thin rugs made of woven maize or plaited palm leaf. All of these have similar sound-deadening qualities to carpet and are much more eco-friendly (a vigorous shaking in the fresh air replaces chemically-based carpet cleaner). Better suited to adults without a family of accident-prone, clumsy/young children,

natural-fibre flooring is known for its capacity to stain and shrink. (If you do have children, the new wool-mix carpets, with a sisal effect in weave and texture, are much easier to maintain.)

Additional Zen flooring options – including bare wood boards, wood laminate, limestone, silvery slate, marble and terracotta – are smooth and understated. These materials are best suited to areas such as hallways, bathrooms and kitchens, where a sleek surface is much more hygienic than fibrous matting. For an ultra-glossy finish, a resin floor painted with three coats of high-gloss polyurethane gives a brilliant effect, particularly in black or white.

Flooring plays a starring role in Zen interiors. Resin tiles coated with high-gloss paint gives a clean streamlined effect (below) **, while natural-fibre matting** (right) **has long-since been the number one flooring for futons.**

Underfloor Heating

Because they live so much of their domestic lives close to the floor, the Japanese are big fans of underfloor heating, which radiates warmth evenly and effectively, and can be laid underneath any type of flooring. In addition, this concept adheres to the Zen ideal of an invisible infrastructure; it is also energy-efficient and a great way to enjoy marble, stone and slate flooring without having to shuffle around in a pair of fluffy slippers – very un-Zen – because of the cold. Rubber flooring is the perfect material for underfloor heating, while the latest technique includes thick wiring, which can be fixed onto any solid floor surface before it is covered with ceramic or stone tiles.

Warmer on the feet and much kinder to your bank balance, are stone-, marble- or slate-effect vinyls. Interior wooden carpets, using a hardwood veneer and laid in the same way as ordinary carpets, are another option, while an increasing number of beautifully-designed radiators, including wall-mounted silver spirals and subtle granite styles are as decorative as they are functional – presenting yet another alternative to ripping up your floors, while still maintaining a minimalist Zen feel.

Low-slung Living

The Japanese relax best by sitting on floor cushions arranged around the 'kotatsu', a low table with a built-in covered heater designed to keep feet warm. Similarly simple seating has been gaining momentum in the West since the 1960s, when Moroccan and Turkish kelim cushions littered the floors of laid-back sitting rooms everywhere. Saggy, baggy Seventies-style beanbags followed, creating a generation of slouchers, whose posture only improved in the 1980s when upright chrome and leather styles were the order of the day.

Taking its cue from the East, contemporary seating has gone to ground once again. In addition to the growing breed of style-conscious hotels and shops which have helped to make floor cushions hot property, the new-look seating is more structured, with cube-shaped pouffes and rectilinear floor cushions taking centre stage. Natural materials – such as suede, leather and alpaca – are counterbalanced by ethnic fabrics, including antique Cambodian wedding silks, cushions panelled with swatches of patterned kimono fabrics and silk plissé in soft metallic shades.

Even beanbags have foregone their formerly floppy shape in favour of a more buoyant approach, while the new inflatable styles can be quickly restored with a few breaths of fresh air. And if the pull of gravity leaves you feeling seriously depressed, low-slung sofas and chairs covered in pristine canvas slips also fit the bill.

As ubiquitous as the three-piece suite in the 1970s, low tables, sofas, chairs, daybeds and fabric-covered cubes are contemporary furniture staples for Westerners keen to swing low. Louche lounging, Eastern style, began with the daybed before dropping down to the perennially popular futon, which is also good for your back. (Note: the Japanese do not suffer from postural problems.)

Whether you use your futon in true Japanese style – laying it on a tatami floor mat or placing it on a raised wooden plinth – this hard, flat mattress, filled with layers of cotton and wool, has become a popular feature in Western interiors, especially with the recent upsurge in space-saving sleeping niches – platforms suspended above another room, and reached by clambering up a ladder.

Above and below

Eschewing their three-piece suites for funky floor cushions and fashionable suede cubes, Westerners are responding to the pull of gravity.

Three Colours White

Lighter Shades of Pale

There are three main strands which make up the Zen colour palette. The first centres around a code of basic neutrals, including white, cream, buff, beige and biscuit. This option appeals to minimalist designers like John Pawson and Philippe Starck (who designed the all-white Delano hotel in Miami). Anouska Hempel, another Zen designer, likes to pick and choose from 65 different shades of white, while Kelly Hoppen has recently launched Perfect Neutrals, a range of paint colours for those who understand the importance of sorting the wheat from the chaff. Clearly, the magnolia years are over: these days purists can sweat over the just-visible differences between antique white, lime white and bone white, not to mention vanilla, ecru, ivory, calico, flax and clay. Sticking to pale colours is ideal for lifestylistas who want to create a harmonious Zen interior with the minimum of fuss. In addition, restricting your palette allows greater freedom with furnishings and decoration, while slashes of colour should be introduced to prevent rooms from looking too flat. It should also be noted that walls painted in pale shades will reflect natural light, making rooms seem bigger and brighter, while continuity of colour prevents fragmentation, giving your home a sense of coherence. Westerners should beware of brilliant white, however, which can be too harsh in colder, northern climates, where the hours of daylight are shorter in winter and the strength of light is dulled by clouds. Warmer cream tones are infinitely preferable.

Colour and Contrast

The second strand in the Zen palette accelerates the pace a notch above neutral; air and water colours such as muted blues, greens, greys, pinks and browns, are interspersed with flashes of navy, turquoise, orange and red. These traditional Zen colours are always present in interior design, thanks to the ancient belief that the five natural elements – earth, water, fire, forest and metal – be represented in your living space for a harmonious sense of order and balance.

The third colourway concentrates on contrast, a feature long-since patronized by the Japanese, who are particularly fond of monochrome. The striking combination of black

Left **Monochrome interiors offer a calming sense of balance and space.**

Everything the same; everything distinct

ZEN PROVERB

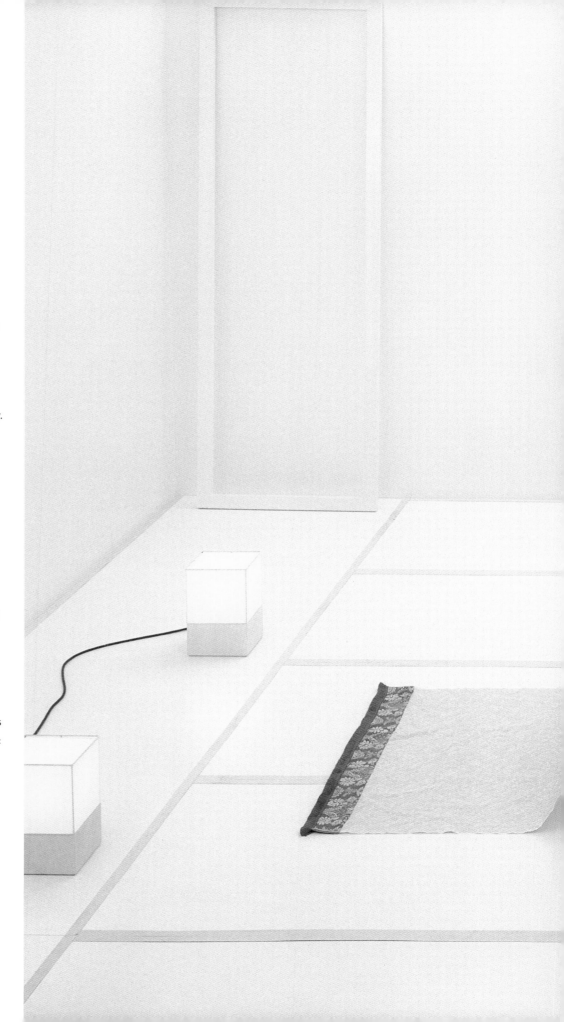

Right **High-gloss floors and all-white furnishings give this pristine interior a sense of weightlessness – while the horizontal bed banner and dark trim of the matting help bring it back down to earth.**

and white is witnessed in Shoji screens, calligraphy wall banners, Isamu Noguchi's famous spider-legged light designs and black-and-white photographs.

Vivid colour contrasts are also an option in the Zen interior, offering a brilliant compromise to those wary about living entirely in the buff. Options include painting one wall scorching pink and leaving the others in neutral, or using a strong colour like red and combining it with a paler one such as celadon for a charge of energy. (If you indulge in this way, however, additional decoration must be strictly monitored.) Even more contemporary, is the three-colour scheme, which it is possible to employ while still maintaining a minimalist look. Three colours – even if they are strong ones – can create a fabulous sense of harmony: the hard part is getting the balance right.

Texture

To prevent minimalist interiors from becoming too bland, texture is a vital feature. Natural fabrics such as leather, suede, camel hair or cashmere soften stark white cubes, helping to balance the hard lines and pure colours of the minimalist look with a luxuriously tactile element. Another way to solve visual dilemmas is to contrast luxury elements with tough ones: team fragile silk with cool-edged concrete, smooth linen with fibrous flooring and fluffy sheepskin with sharp shapes.

Textural contrasts even work for those committed purists who are unwilling to break the continuity of their all-white interiors. 'Texture is the new colour,' declares Kelly Hoppen, a designer who uses up to seven fabrics – including chenille, velvet and damask – in the same colour in order to prevent single-shade interiors from appearing too spartan.

Beauty springs from thought and sensibility rather than from material wealth CLAUDIO SILVESTRIN

Lightening Up

Maximizing natural light is very important in Eastern interiors. As a result, windows are kept clear inside and out – with light-blocking furniture, heavy drapes and window boxes a definite no-no. Instead, the Japanese dress their windows with electric panels, Canto screens, roller blinds pierced with tiny holes, translucent linen curtains and Venetian slats, all of which allow light to be harnessed.

City dwellers, or anyone nervous about being overlooked by neighbours, should invest in some bottom-up Roman blinds, which guarantee privacy as well as allowing light to penetrate. Floor-to-ceiling sliding glass doors have long been used in Zen design, while contemporary options include skylights and atriums. Both of these provide good and constant sources of light, as opposed to standard windows, where the amount of light varies according to the season, weather and time of day.

Light amplifies your space, and as far as electric lighting is concerned, the Zen approach is subtle but efficient. In a traditional Japanese room, light is harnessed to create dramatic contrasts: dark areas are balanced by light ones, and overhead lighting – generally thought to be too harsh and impersonal – is replaced by uplighters or table lamps (try clear, hand-blown glass bases with organza shades in oyster or pearl). Paper lamps in cubes, cones, beehives and circles also offer an ambient light effect and have been a ubiquitous feature in Japanese households since the advent of Isamu Noguchi's designs in the mid-twentieth century. Wall-mounted lights are also favoured in Zen decorating circles, providing an effective alternative to keeping surfaces clean and

clear, while low-hanging pendant lamps in sets of two or three are perfect for illuminating a low bench or drawers placed either side of a low bed. Choose simple, small glass or white ceramic shades, with black or white flexes.

If lights are wired to circuits operated from a single panel with a dimmer switch, you can operate and control them from the same base. This adheres to the clutter-free principles of Zen living by reducing the need for ugly sockets, plugs and trailing wires. However, if you want to make use of a whole range of lighting – table, wall and floor – putting everything on a single switch is a mistake. To create a range of moods, lights should be fitted with bulbs of varying wattage and controlled by individual circuits.

Spatial Discipline

The modern fusion of East and West centres on spatial discipline. The Japanese believe that inspiration should come from rooms where the proportions, space and light create the decoration. As a result, contemporary Zen interiors should create an efficient flow of energizing chi, best achieved by knocking through as many walls as possible (replacing load-bearing walls with pillars) to maximize space and air and create an airy open-plan feel.

Another way to make your home appear more spacious is to arrange the furniture so that it looks balanced. Sofas, chairs and tables should be spread out to allow plenty of air to flow between each piece, as well as maintain a clear passageway from one side of the room to the other. Not only does this allow you to traverse your space with ease, it also helps to make rooms look bigger.

Left **Free-flowing space is essential in Zen interiors. Sliding doors and long runners stretching between rooms maximizes a feeling of fluidity.**

Three Colour White

Zoning

If you have wooden floors it's easy to delineate an area such as your dining quarter or work space with a rug or mat. Hailed by interior decorators as 'the next big thing', patterned, coloured or neutral rugs should be used as a contextual centrepiece, so that the surrounding floorboards serve as free-flowing walkways which lead to separate living entities. If you're planning to remove doors in order to give your space more of an open-plan feel, a single step or an opaque glass screen will both work as subtle dividing devices.

Inner Sanctums

The Japanese love to create a room within a room – and using a screen to create an inner sanctum has long been a part of their decorating vocabulary. Traditionally used to wash and dress behind, screens are great delineators of space, and can be moved around to create varying configurations within a room. Modern alternatives to paper shoji screens – a favourite in Eastern interiors – include lightweight, portable ones (which can be folded up and put away when not in use), mobile room dividers (with shelves one side for extra storage) and dual-function bookcases (which can be elongated to divide space).

Sliding doors are also great space enhancers, as are translucent bricks or sandblasted glass panels. Semi-opaque glass reflects light back into a room, as well as adding a degree of privacy, while alternative translucent materials include fibreglass, plastic, resin and Perspex. The best option, of course, is mirrored glass, which creates a fabulous illusion of space and light,

especially when it is positioned to reflect a blank wall or window (effectively doubling the amount of light). Materials such as stainless steel and marble, are also light reflective and these surfaces work particularly well in bathrooms, thanks to their shimmery, watery appearance.

Multifunctional Furniture

When planning a minimalist space, everything you own has to work twice as hard to justify its existence. As a result, multifunctional furniture is a godsend, especially for small interiors. Starting with the sofa bed and progressing to shelves which extend up to three times their length, contemporary furniture designers are doing backflips in the adaptability stakes: tables become chairs, chairs extend into benches, coffee tables transform themselves into a mini-home office and nests of occasional tables spawn smaller, identical versions, which can be tucked away at the end of the day.

Clothes rails on castors, stools which hang on the wall and collapsible furniture also help to make the most of your space, while modular bathroom storage – in the shape of chrome metal rails used to support cabinets, hook soap dishes and encompass storage units – are becoming increasingly popular. Multifunctionability is also about using your furniture imaginatively, so that your leather floor cubes work as a seat, a footstool or a table (if you clump cubes together); and your bamboo ladder functions as a rail for drying clothes, or a rack for hanging towels.

Above left **Demonstrating the subtle ingenuity of multifunctional furniture, this bedside chest by Japanese design duo, the Azumi's, elongates into an elegant coffee table.**
Right **Create an inner sanctum using smooth-sliding walls.**

Three Colours White

Cleansing Rituals

Americans bathe to get clean, Japanese clean to bathe ANCIENT TRUISM

Right **Communal bathing is still practised by Japanese families today.**
Far right **A single wall-mounted tap and spherical stone sink are all that's required for Japanese-style abluting.**

The Japanese are a meticulous race and nowhere is this more apparent than in their bathing rituals. Viewing Western-style ablutions as laughable – why would anyone wanting a clean body wallow in their own grimy bathwater? – the Japanese wash in two stages: phase one involves a thorough body scrub in the shower; phase two, a leisurely soak in a deep, wooden tub until the body is relaxed and the mind rejuvenated.

This obsession with bathing is one of the few aspects of Japanese culture which does not have its roots in China. Instead, the national passion for water stems from the country's many volcanic springs, some of which are rich in minerals and others which permeate the air with the scent of hibiscus and pine. In addition, both Shinto and Buddhist teachings preach religious purification through immersion, allowing the Japanese the luxury of regular, guilt-free wallowing.

With all beings I wash body and mind free from dust, pure and shining within and without
A SIGN AT THE ENTRANCE TO A HOT SPRING IN JAPAN

Right **Austere bathroom fixtures and fittings create a clutter-free environment in which to rejuvenate body and soul.**

No one knows exactly when the Japanese first started to use their hot springs for bathing, but legend connects certain spas with the aquatic antics of ancient gods, and such sites are still recognized as sacred. Today, these spas are patronized by curious tourists and Gucci-toting geishas alike, and are legendary for their ability to promote relaxation. Communal wallowing is also practised in the contemporary Japanese home: children usually bathe with one parent, and a group backscrub is customary, with every family member benefiting from regular exfoliation. This is followed by a brisk shower before the process of restoring your mental and physical health (i.e. a long soak) begins.

Designed for more than one person, the traditional Japanese 'furo', or wooden bath, is shorter than its Western counterpart and deep enough to allow water to cover the shoulders of a seated person. The water is used for soaking only and can therefore be shared by several people, one after the other. This economical approach is compounded by the tub's smaller surface area, which allows water to stay hotter for longer. Water heat is further conserved by placing a wooden lid over the bath between users.

The Japanese ritual of purification is reflected in the refined details of traditional bath-house design, where austerity and simplicity is employed in the pursuit of visual calm. Possessions are kept out of view, except for a plant such as a fern or orchid, which helps the bather to keep in touch with nature. Plumbing pipes are invisible, and taps and faucets are often plugged into a facing wall so that bath or basin edges remain uncluttered.

Washing in the West

Procuring a contemporary Zen bathroom is a
simple process: just stick to a strict minimalist
code like Philippe Starcke and John Pawson
and you can't go wrong. Aesthetically, these
designers have passed the litmus test: both
bathe in spare monastic rooms, where the
plumbing is invisible, the use of materials
natural and the dedication to water absolute.
However, neither room features the essential
pre-bath shower. Philippe Starck's water room
at his country retreat has a freestanding, old-
fashioned looking basin and roll-top bath,
both of which appear to have little regard for
plumbing. In fact, the underground waterworks

enable him to furnish his bathroom with
the sort of spontaneity normally reserved
for the sitting room.

Taking his cue from traditional Japanese tubs,
John Pawson has dedicated his bathroom to the
enjoyment of water. Wanting to free the mind
from distraction, while natural materials and
an abundance of hot water generate a sense of
wellbeing, his deep, stone tub can be filled to
overflowing, with water spilling onto the floor and
draining away through a grid of stones. The basin
is a hemisphere shape scooped out of a solid cube
of stone (complete with essential wall-mounted
tap), and the WC is concealed in a bench.

Right and below **Wood, stone, or marble are ideal materials for creating a Japanese bathroom, but for the ultimate Zen water room make sure that lotions and potions are neatly stashed away behind closed doors.**

Those lacking in watery inspiration should look to the world's hippest hotels for a variety of refreshing ideas. Frequently spartan, but always equipped with excellent plumbing, spotless linen and luxury cosmetics, bathrooms in chic, boutique hotels like the W in Seattle and the Mercer in New York illustrate the wisdom of keeping to the white stuff. Designed by Christian Liaigre in his signature combination of dark African wenge wood, reflective marble surfaces and white mosaic walls, Mercer bathrooms also have a Zen-style alcove set above the massive square bath, which is big enough for a single-stem flower vase.

Left **The fashion for painting one wall in a strong colour and leaving the others plain is an effective minimalist technique.** Below and right **Wooden accessories and a cup of Sake to sip while you soak complete the Japanese bathing experience.**

Black-and-white tiled floors also have Zen overtones, and were originally inspired by French interior designer Andrée Putman, who created the monochrome bathrooms at the Morgan Hotel in New York. Alternative materials for contemporary Zen bathrooms include stainless steel, limestone, marble or concrete bleached to a pale dove grey. Glass is another option worth considering; after all, what could be more purifying than a gleaming glass bath, placed on a glass floor, flanked by glass wall tiles? (Faux glass tiles offer a shatterproof alternative.)

Earthy types who can afford to buy a Japanese wooden tub should opt for cedar or cypress woods as both release aromatic odours when they come into contact with water. A square, teak sink is a less expensive option, while treated pine decking or bamboo floors will appeal to naturalists as both are one hundred per cent waterproof, and work particularly well in shower cubicles.

Details

Little touches can also contribute to the Zen bathing experience. Set the tone with wooden soap dishes, toothmugs and bath racks, or try a bobbly bathmat bound in Abaca, which offers Shiatsu for feet. In addition, washing with a bar of bamboo salt soap (very popular in Japan), will help to make you slimmer according to its marketing campaign, while sipping a cup of sake as you soak is a pleasurably decadent habit widely practised in Japan.

New Order

Those who want the fewest things are nearest to the gods SOCRATES

Left **Keeping tabs on your clutter is much easier when your storage solutions are appealing. These Japanese boxes are begging to be filled with treasured possessions such as photographs, letters and postcards.**

Storage can be Sexy

The philosophy of clearing your space, and hence your mind, is one that works for most people. According to the Japanese way of thinking, clutter is a stagnant feature, blocking chi (or essential energy) which could be put to better use elsewhere. Not only do too many possessions require an overkill on the dusting front, but being late for an important interview because your car keys were hidden under a pile of unopened bills is an unneccesary hassle. Better by far, is getting to the interview with five minutes for reflection.

Many people view sorting through their stuff – and keeping it sorted – as the domain of the anally retentive. To them, labelling shoeboxes or sticking photographs into albums signals the advent of obsessive behaviour, but this is not necessarily the case. Certainly, there are some people who find it difficult to function unless they know where everything is, but deciding to edit your possessions does not mean that you are about to turn into a humourless control freak.

Deep down, we'd all like our homes to look clean, clear, and bright – and storing and concealing items will help to achieve this. Edit your possessions once, and you will find that keeping your home clutter-free soon becomes second nature. In addition, you will a) be amazed by the amount of time you can save once you know where everything is and b) discover just how much you can get rid of without even noticing its absence.

Out of Sight, Out of Mind

Before you start on your storage crusade, you must first of all prune your possessions. Generally, clutter is of the mindless variety: sofas are stacked with too many cushions; magazine racks bulge with old sections of the Sunday newspapers; files are stuffed with bills dating back to the 1980s, and clothes rails groan under the weight of things you will never wear again.

The answer to all this, as any professional organizer will tell you, is to divide your possessions up into four piles: pile one is for clothes and items you no longer want. (These can either be donated to charity or sold at a second-hand shop.) Pile two is for things you want to store, pile three is for those possessions you cannot live without, and pile four is for rubbish. The focus should be on functionability, but editing your possessions does not mean you must restrict yourself to basics. Living without personal knick-knacks is a soul-less exercise, and while dedicated purists assert that your home should only be filled with objects are both necessary and beautiful, we all have sentimental mementoes – attractive or otherwise – which demand to be displayed.

Large Storage Solutions

The key to minimal living is good cupboards (this way you can stash your clutter without having to resort to overkill on the bin-bag front). If possible, opt for built-in storage, which takes up less space than freestanding pieces, as well as presenting a streamlined effect. A perennial favourite with minimalists, built-in cupboards which have been panelled or papered to match the room are ideal for disguising a plethora of possessions. Keep lines clean with cleverly designed pop-open cupboards (which allow you to dispense with door handles altogether), or flush-fit door pulls.

Alternative solutions include structural storage that fits into the framework of your space. This is achieved by replacing partition walls with floor-to-ceiling storage systems which are accessible from both sides, or by adding a parallel wall next to an existing one to create storage space between them. Modular units with a mix of open-and-shut storage are a similarly nifty alternative (architectural holes in the wall present additional space for books, magazines, ornaments and electrical equipment).

Space-saving shelving should be kept tight to the wall and, where possible, recessed to maintain a streamlined look. A low platform on wheels can create valuable storage by utilizing the space under the bed, while a sectional rattan sofa, with capacious chests forming the base of each unit, offers additional space for bedding, sportsgear and toys. The shallow drawers of an art-school plan chest are excellent for keeping collections of belts, hankies and scarves, while space-conscious desks with swing-out work areas and a pedestal stand to keep PC towers out of the way, are essential for cramped home offices. Combining storage with a display area is another unique way of cutting down on clutter as both requirements are fulfilled by a single piece of furniture; the Oriental answer to this is a simple, wooden wedding chest.

Anti-clockwise, from left
**Stash your clutter
in a choice of wicker
stairbaskets, silk bags
from Vietnam or nifty
sisal pots.**
Right **Arranged along
slim streamlined shelving,
kitchen paraphernalia can
make an attractive display.**

Small Storage Solutions

Many ethnic storage ideas originate from ancient cultures, where portable carriers were geared towards itinerant lifestyles. Today, these solutions are fashionable as well as functional, with stacking baskets from Japan, camphor chests from China, wicker laundry bins from Thailand and sisal baskets from Vietnam.

A natural alternative to the streamlined look, woven containers – from rattan to bamboo – are available in all shapes and sizes, with sisal at the forefront of the trend for natural-looking storage. Made from the leaves of the Agave plant, and available in numerous different colours and patterns, sisal baskets provide an attractive yet practical way to store a wide variety of items, from cosmetics in the bathroom to pot-pourri on a window sill and socks and scarves in the wardrobe.

Other small storage solutions include wall-mounted magazine racks, hanging sweater and shoe stores, overdoor organizers, complete with numerous nifty pockets, folding plate racks, junk-drawer organizers, laundry baskets designed to tuck neatly into the corner of a room, and wrought-iron wine tables with bottle racks arranged in vertical order down the base.

Decanting

The smart solution to bulky boxes and ugly packaging is to decant the contents the moment you unpack your shopping basket. This is particularly pertinent in kitchens, where dry goods such as pasta, rice and cereals can easily be stored in attractive glass jars. A similar process also applies in bathrooms, where a row of simple white pots, artfully arranged on a plain glass shelf, makes a decorative feature of mundane items such as cotton-wool balls and hair rollers. Combining form with function, the art of decanting adheres to the primary Zen principle of creating beauty out of necessity.

3 Nature admits no lie

JANE WELSH CARLYLE

The relationship between man and nature is at the forefront of Far Eastern philosophies, especially in Thailand, Indonesia and Japan, where the boundaries between outside and in are purposefully sketchy. The Thais and Indonesians favour airy, open-plan 'salas' and 'bales', while sliding glass doors opening onto gardens and courtyards have always been a dominant feature of Japanese architecture. In the West our approach to housing is quite different, thanks to the vagaries of the weather. Instead of balmy temperatures, we have to batten the hatches against icy winds and sleeting rain, and thus distance ourselves from the natural environment. But communing with nature does not necessarily mean we should relocate to a tropical island, or even go around hugging trees. A carefully tended window box, or a room furnished with natural materials and lots of plants will satisfy our need to connect with nature. Even if you live in the heart of a big city, there are myriad ways of bringing the outside in.

The move towards using natural materials in the home began in the early 1990s, with imports from the Far East becoming the mainstay of chic interiors shops across Europe and the USA. Bamboo furniture from Indonesia, traditional textiles from Vietnam and decorative wood carvings from Thailand all flooded Western markets, while home-grown products range from organic paint to hemp wallpaper and clover-print carpets.

Outside In

Furniture design has also gone green; straight lines and orthodox shapes have been replaced by tables and chairs that follow nature's design rather than man's. In accordance with this relaxed approach, homes can be furnished in an imaginative off-beat style, with trees spreading their branches into brightly-lit skywells, and indoor water features tinkling merrily. In addition, contemporary architects are more than happy to tear down walls and enlarge windows in a bid to create airy, open-plan spaces – the new look for modern interiors, which takes its cue from Eastern building styles.

These days, back-to-basics has a good deal more style than its earlier inception during the 1970s, when tatty rattan bookcases buckled under the weight of Sister Sledge records and ornamental grasses rustled in suburban gardens. In the new millennium, hippie caneware has been replaced by textured wood, and the ubiquitous cheeseplant by sculptural *fritillaria*. Accordingly, the new, loose-limbed living style requires lots of home entertaining: after all, what's the point in having Gucci's beautiful, bamboo-handled cutlery, or Calvin Klein's tableware range – available in an organic palette of earthy colours – if you can't show them off?

This chapter takes a look at contemporary interiors with a natural bent. Open House describes the merits of creating an airy space, perfect for the plethora of natural materials discussed in Natural Selection. Falling Water underlines the importance of going with the flow, while New Organic concentrates on sculptural plants for the home and describes how to re-create a Zen garden in your own backyard.

Open House

Housing in Bali and Thailand

In a bid to connect as much as possible with the environment, bigger, brighter and lighter have become the defining features of interiors in the twenty-first century. There is no better example of this than the open-plan architecture of traditional Balinese housing. Designed to reflect the form of its inhabitants, with the head represented by the ancestral shrine, the arms by the living and sleeping quarters, and the legs and feet by the kitchen and rice granaries, homes on Bali offer a harmonious setting that is as much in tune with its inhabitants, as it is with the environment that surrounds it.

The purest example of Indonesian housing has to be the Amandari, a luxurious hotel on the island of Bali. Designed by architect Peter Muller, Amandari represents the layout of a typical Balinese village, and uses indigenous materials for a look that manages to be both traditional and contemporary. Instead of the room-lined corridors of conventional hotels, each guest stays in their own private pavilion, which is enclosed by a stone wall and forms a secluded mini-compound. The pavilions themselves stand 9 m (30 ft) tall, and are built from teak and volcanic stone. The roofs are thatched in ylang ylang grass and supported by lashed bamboo resting on bamboo columns. In the main area of the hotel, the traditional low-hanging roofs of the long halls are flanked by rustling palms and giant vases of scented frangipani flowers, while gleaming Indonesian marble slabs and smooth teak daybeds contrast with rough-cut limestone pavers and ancient Hindu sculptures bedecked with colourful floral garlands.

With every rising of the sun think of your life as just begun

ELLA WHEELER WILCOX

Above and right **Above and right Introduce nature into your home with frondy wallpapers, or create a window which overlooks a leafy vista.** Overleaf **Jerôme Abel Séguin's home on the Indonesian island of Sumbawa is a showcase for his organic sculptures, which are hewn from hunks of found wood.**

In Thailand, creating spacious housing along the lines of the architecture of ancient kingdoms is also part of the culture. This is exemplified by the Sukhotai hotel in Bankok, which takes its inspiration from the sumptuous palaces of Siam. Palatial in size, the super-luxurious hotel is pervaded by the exotic scents of jasmine and tuberose. Cool, covered walkways are flanked by brass lampholders and terracotta frames inserted into the plastered walls, while Thai silk upholstery complements the occasional bronze Buddha.

Similarly, the Amanpuri hotel on the southern island of Phuket is based on a stylized temple complex, inspired by Ayutthya, the ancient capital of Thailand. Built using local granite and hardwoods, the hotel's 40 private guest pavilions are set on a palm-studded hillside and each is loosely divided into separate areas for sitting, lounging, reading, sleeping and bathing. Teak floors, white walls and rugged pieces of indigenous art create a minimalist look that combines grand monumentalism with ethnic modernism.

Communing with Nature

Being at one with the natural world is not an entirely Eastern prerogative. For the past decade, French sculptor Jérôme Abel Seguin has spent eight months of the year on Sumbawa – an island in the Indonesian archipelago – where he makes monolithic chairs and tables from hunks of found wood. Originally inspired by the raw environment of the island, the former window-dresser kicked off his sculpting career after presenting Louis Vuitton with a bag of driftwood, débris and rattan chicken coops picked up on his first visit. Vuitton loved the organic slant, decorating the windows of their Parisian shop with Seguin's booty. Today, the sculptor's natural pieces are still very much in demand, thanks to an ever-increasing list of homeowners desperate to introduce the elemental landscape of Sumbawa into their homes.

On an even grander scale, Russel Wright, the late American architect, designed his house to form part of the cliffs which hug the Hudson river, 50 miles north of Manhattan. Adhering to the Oriental concept of 'shibui' (or under-statement), the simple, organic structure has an indoor waterfall, sliding glass windows and a door decorated with ferns, flowers and butterflies pressed under plastic laminate. Even the light from sunbeams and moon glow has been taken into account, an attractive option liable to cause non-architects overpowering feelings of envy. However, it is possible to turn your home into a nature sanctuary, even if you can't afford to include the waxing of the moon and the rising of the sun as part of your design.

Details

Being able to see into the outside world is essential for homeowners who want to connect with the natural environment. Aside from increasing the number and size of your windows, implementing skylights and conservatories allows communion with the great outdoors as well as increasing all-essential light options. Mirrored screens that reflect the outside into the interior are another way to bring the outside in, while sliding glass doors also blur the boundaries, especially if the exterior flooring is in the same material as that of the interior. For those restricted by a tight budget or strict planning regulations, digitally-produced wallpaper depicting clouds, twilight or night skies is a great alternative to the real thing, as is painting your ceiling with clouds or decorating a bed canopy with stars. Contemporary flooring also offers a multitude of natural-looking choices – from grass-effect rugs to tiles patterned with pebbles or deep-blue water (instantly recalling the pristine depths of paradise islands, such as Koh Samui and Koh Pha-Ngan in Thailand).

The spacious firmament on high with all the blue ethereal sky

JOSEPH ADDISON

If you live in an urban environment with no outside space, connect with the great outdoors by creating your own personal skyscape. These atmospheric wallpapers (below) are a great way to make even the smallest interiors appear to extend into the depths of infinity.

Left **The immediacy of this panoramic photowall makes you wonder why there is no sound of tumbling water: faking it has never looked so good.**

Elemental furnishings also link a house with its surroundings. Garden furniture offers an attractive alternative to standard indoor styles. Luxe-up decorative wrought-iron benches, slatted wooden chairs or wicker loungers with richly upholstered cushions and super-soft throws.

Another idea is to re-create the feeling of balmy Eastern nights by draping your bed with floaty muslin folds falling from a corona fixed to the ceiling. Windows dressed with fine blinds made from undyed hessian or vetiver are also

reminiscent of the Far East – as are flimsy, cotton curtains which puff out in the gentlest of breezes like spindly bamboo slats wafting in the trade winds of the tropics.

Panoramic photowalls depicting gushing waterfalls, mountain ranges or steamy rainforests instantly transform your home into a natural haven – as do shag-pile rugs in varying hues of grassy green, shower curtains patterned with pretty wild-flower designs and bedlinen bristling with bamboo. Even super-fake Astroturf will do the trick.

Natural Selection

Wood

These days homeowners with natural leanings are spoilt for choice. With dozens of different types of stone, natural weaves and textured wallcoverings available, making nature an integral part of your life is simply a matter of choice. First off the blocks is wood, the most fashionable furnishing option as far as contemporary designers are concerned, thanks to its versatility, durability and enormous variety of colour, texture and grain.

For the contemporary Eastern look, tropical timbers are the ones to choose: teak, mango wood and Burmese rosewood (all known for their aromatic charms and warm, earthy appearance) are ideal for large pieces of furniture such as beds, dining tables and ornately-carved sofas. More organic, still, is the furniture made by villagers in north-west Vietnam, where tables and chairs are made from tree roots, and stools are hewn from untreated chunks of ekki. Moreover, it is possible to consolidate the rustic look by finishing your dining-room table with delicate Indonesian teasets fashioned out of slivers of bark.

Left **Thanks to its versatility, durability and aesthetic appeal, wood is the most fashionable furnishing option in contemporary interiors, with organic-shaped furniture first off the blocks.**

Below **An all-wood
bedroom combines
an ethnic carving with
a modern cube table.
The chair, inspired by
Frank O Gehry's Easy
Edges range, is made
from cardboard and
folds back on itself in
seductive sinuous rolls.**

The strength of a tree that connects with the earth yet reaches for the sky

REI KAWAKUBO

Below **An all-wood
bedroom combines
an ethnic carving with
a modern cube table.
The chair, inspired by
Frank O Gehry's Easy
Edges range, is made
from cardboard and
folds back on itself in
seductive sinuous rolls.**

Natural Selection

Bamboo and Rattan

Probably the Far East's best-known import, bamboo is viewed in the West as the new über wood. Naturally sustainable as well as light, waterproof and attractive, bamboo-framed houses with bamboo matt walls are a common sight across China. In addition, according to the ancient philosophy of feng shui, a fresh bunch of bamboo augers good luck, bringing health, wealth and prosperity. Bamboo is also popular in Japan, where over 1,000 reported uses for it include bridge-building, furniture-making and the crafting of cookware.

As far as the contemporary Eastern look is concerned, bamboo is an easy way to 'naturalize' your home with an attendant flick of exotica. Moreover, its inexpensive price tag allows homeowners to indulge their natural instincts as fully as they wish. Choose from square planters, lightweight screens and elegant bedheads, or go for a more delicate approach with bamboo lamps, cutlery, trays and coatstands. Raw bamboo canes can also be fashioned into clothes rails and shoe racks (simply cut the poles to the appropriate length and bind them together with leather string or raffia), while traditional bamboo ladders are a natural alternative to chrome towel racks.

Wide lengths of bamboo, cut into sections, also make attractive soap dishes, candlesticks or containers for pens and pencils. (A length of bamboo consists of long, hollow sections divided by thin areas of wood, which can be identified by the distinctive horizontal lines or notches on the bamboo. To ensure your container has a base, saw through the bamboo just below one of these notches and then smooth the edge with a sheet of fine sandpaper.)

Left **The merits of bamboo are almost too numerous to list. A naturally sustainable wood, it is strong, durable, waterproof and versatile – not to mention light, attractive and cost-effective.**

Rattan is another eco-friendly wood which is also gaining popularity on the contemporary home front. A palm rather than a grass, the most common rattans are species of Calamus found in the Malay peninsular as well as Vietnam and Indonesia. Offering a lightweight alternative to sturdier furnishings in the form of blinds, magazine racks and CD storage units, rattan joins coconut wood (either left matt or flecked with dark patches) and palmwood as textural options to light woods such as beech and cherry – which can both look a bit bland.

As a modern alternative to the traditional rustic look, cardboard offers the perfect solution. Inspired by Frank O Gehry's 'Easy Edges' range, cardboard chairs which curve back on themselves in sinuous folds are sleek and sexy, while Japanese designer Shigeru Ban's tubular range (originally based on a design for a post-earthquake shelter) is also crafted out of cardboard. In addition, shops such as Muji offer a plethora of furniture and accessories made out of cardboard, including wheelie storage chests, flatpack drawers and wastepaper bins.

Furniture aside, wood panelling on walls and ceilings is a great way to 'naturalize' contemporary interiors. Easy to effect, the best option is textural tongue-and-groove, which recalls wind-blown beaches lined with brightly-painted changing huts. Most commonly used to box in baths and unattractive pipework, tongue-and-groove wall cladding can be used to cover up a multitude of other horrors – from woodchip wallpaper to unsightly damp patches. Paint it in a strong, glossy emulsion, or leave it raw for a warm, rustic feel: either way, the linearity of the textured planks has a calming effect, helping to create a simple rustic haven with an earthy Eastern feel.

Far left **A tall bamboo frame and woven-leaf basket provide great bathroom storage.**
Left **Natural leanings – CDs are neatly stacked in a bamboo tower.**
Right **Pebble floor tiles give traditional stone flooring a funky contemporary twist.**

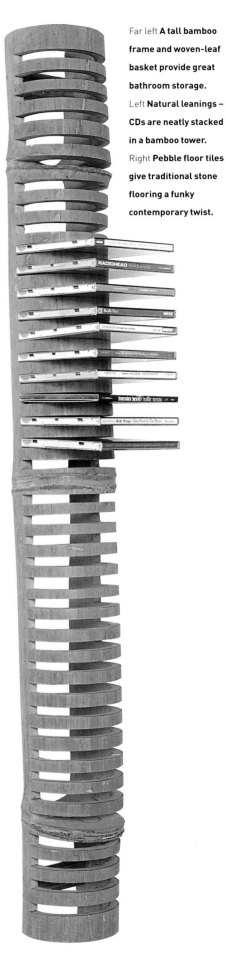

Stone

Since prehistoric times, stone has been used
as the strongest and most enduring of building
materials. Natural rock caves are the earliest
dwelling places we know of, and while stone
flooring has always been a consistent feature in
interior design, its return to the limelight is due
to a raft of designer shops and hotels paving their
floors in soft stone slabs. From Calvin Klein in
New York to Vong restaurant at the Berkeley
hotel in London (where diners eat off square- or
round-shaped limestone tables), the versatility
and beauty of stone is once again in evidence.
Capable of appearing coolly inviting or warm
and earthy, stone's appearance improves with
age, although sadly it is also expensive. For those
unable to indulge on a grand scale, a few details
will work wonders. Choose from decorative stone
balls, stone door knobs, lava dishes, limestone
sinks or baths and tableware. Even a handful
of pebbles in a glass bowl will look the part.

Left **Wallpaper printed
with sticks of bamboo is
a popular contemporary
Eastern design.**
Below **Try hanging a
single strip of paper
like a banner for a
striking organic effect.**

Left **Wallpaper printed
with sticks of bamboo is
a popular contemporary
Eastern design.**
Below **Try hanging a
single strip of paper
like a banner for a
striking organic effect.**

Wallcoverings

From hessian matting to horsehair blinds and side tables fashioned from rope, natural weaves are a great way to bring texture into the home. The current favourite is hemp – an indomitable green crop, whose strong fibres can be spun into fine threads suitable for soft furnishings. Hemp wallpaper is also popular, joining raffia and knobbly grasscloth for a truly textural result. Alternatively, wood-effect wallpaper, complete with genuine-looking whorls, is another option. Choose from blond ash to seductive wenge – and any shade inbetween – as an alternative to the vast number of Eastern-inspired designs, which include bamboo shoots and flower prints.

For homeowners concerned about the environment, organic paint offers an eco-friendly option. A soft and chalky alternative to mass-produced emulsions (which can cause walls to 'suffocate' due to the fungicides and acrylics used to bind them together), natural paints are milk-, water-, plant- or mineral-based, and rely on porous materials such as cassein, chalk and essential oils to help walls 'breathe'. Organic paint also absorbs light, offering a softer and more natural effect.

Texture

The smooth, stone surfaces and strong lines of natural interiors demand textural contrasts. Go against the grain and contrast rough driftwood with cotton-smooth Indonesian batik, and raw materials with lots of glass and silk. Similarly, untreated woods look great beside glossy varieties such as ebony, while cool tactile leather contrasts with warm, tropical styles. Silk plissé, raffia cushions and wickerwork also present a good choice of textural contrasts, especially if they are set against age-old limestone or treated concrete.

Decorative accessories such as the shell drawer handles (below), textural wicker trunk (bottom left) and palmwood salad servers (left) illustrate the myriad ways you can introduce natural elements into the home.

Details

With furniture design riding the organic wave, decorative accessories have followed suit. These days, cushions look naked unless they are fringed with shells or beads, while mirrors are veneered in coconut shell and jostle with terracotta light pulls and crackle-glaze door knobs. Wacky Western designs include Astroturf armchairs, grass-patterned cushions, wooden phones and grooved Zen-garden rugs. For wall decorations, lithographs of shells, plants and palms all fit the bill – as do sheets of split bamboo and workaday items like palmwood salad servers and banana-leaf placemats.

Above right and right
Delicate mother-of-pearl buttons are one way of jazzing up cushion covers, together with exotic beading. Additional decorative accessories include raffia fringing, tinkly bells and delicate shell trims.

Water which is too pure has no fish

TS'AI KEN T'AN

Left **Water from the top tier of the swimming pool at Amankila hotel on Bali creates an endless overflow into the two pools below it.**
Right **This sleek shower cubicle mixes natural materials with modern technology. The sand-blasted glass bricks allow for privacy, in addition to absorbing light from the sky-blue wall opposite, while water from a primitive wooden bowl gushes from a giant overhead shower head.**

Falling Water

Since time began, the sound of running water has soothed troubled spirits. Known across the world for its spiritual and remedial properties, the power of flowing water is particularly pertinent in Eastern philosophies, where it is thought to carry the force of chi (energy and vitality) essential for life. In addition, advocates of feng shui view water in the home as a sure way to activate wealth, while fish – especially carp – symbolize abundance. The Chinese and Japanese also love water lilies, which represent purity and wholesomeness – while reflecting pools in Thailand symbolize peace and serenity, helping the meditative powers of those who gaze into their depths.

Falling water is also predominant in Eastern culture. At Amankila (another Balinese resort in the Aman chain), American architect Ed Tuttle cut three swimming pools into an impossibly steep hill overlooking the Lombok Strait. Cantilevered one above the other, water drips from the top pool into the one below it, and from there into pool number three, where the overflow appears to cascade onto an isolated beach, hundreds of metres below. Amankila is not the only Balinese hotel to have a falling water feature: guests at Begawan Giri bathe in a series of plunge pools fed by a gushing waterfall, while those at Amanwana on the Indonesian island of Moyo need only twist a rock to turn on a waterfall-style shower.

Bathing Au Naturel

Bathing is an essential part of life in the Far East. At every Aman resort across Thailand and Indonesia, the largest space in each guest pavilion is given over to washing, while outdoor baths at Amankila are scattered with rose and frangipani petals, and surrounded by trees full of madly croaking frogs. Californians are also big on natural cleansing rooms. At her home in Malibu, Tatjana Patiz has based her

Water Features

Outdoor

bathroom around the steamy atmosphere of a tropical rainforest. 'I wanted the feel of an outdoor bathroom with all the natural elements,' says the supermodel, whose bamboo-lined shower flanks a deep bath decorated with shells and surrounded by foliage.

Sadly, in colder Western climes, bathing *alfresco* is not always practical, although a freestanding shower with a latticed teak base is quick and easy to erect. Better still, plant a patch of fast-growing bamboo for the sake of privacy, and peeping toms will find their view is obscured in next to no time.

Alternatively, install a skylight above your shower to create a sunlit, starlit or moonlit cubicle, depending on what time of day you prefer to ablute. The best example is John Pawson's sky shower, which has a glass roof that rolls back in summer to create the feeling of cleansing *alfresco*. 'Because there's so much glass, one is very aware of light changes and nature,' says the architect. 'The sun makes the most amazing patterns. On a bright day the whole place glows.'

Not only are water features supposed to bring exceptional financial luck according to the philosophy of feng shui, but the sound of flowing water is renowned for its ability to induce feelings of calm. Moreover, creating your own water feature is not particularly difficult. All you need to do is improvise with anything which can be adapted to house the nozzle of a water jet – sculptures and *objets trouvés*, such as shells or pebbles set into a stone pot, are ideal. Remember, though, that the sound of bubbling or gushing water in an enclosed space, such as a city courtyard, bounces off the walls of the garden or house and can become intrusive. Instead, install a water feature which has a light, tinkling quality rather than one that splashes all over the place. If space is limited, features such as a brimming basin, terracotta urn or bird bath can also be effective. Wall-mounted fountains are also good for small spaces as they can be installed on a balcony or in a conservatory. Use a bamboo spout to enhance the Oriental look.

Outdoor water features also look magical at night. Light a pond the right way and the shadows of your fish will appear on the walls. Failing that, a sunken channel of glass bricks lit from below gives a similar effect to water and also looks stunning when the sun goes down.

Indoor

Indoor water features are another way to introduce movement into your living space. Whether you opt for an expensive design, such as jets of water cascading down a black concrete wall, or a simple, stainless steel cube with water flowing over the sides, is up to you. Basic indoor water features are easy to effect: simply place a mini submersible water pump in a large glass vase or tank. Carefully add stones and shells, positioning them so that the pump is hidden. Fill almost to the brim with water (bottled is best as it won't leave limescale marks), ensuring that the pump is fully submerged. Switch the pump on and adjust the flow of water according to the manufacturer's instructions.

Aquariums

In feng shui tradition, fish have always brought good luck: place a tank in the north corner of your living room and watch your career prospects escalate. It is also advisable to keep nine goldfish – eight red or golden, and one black – to activate the best feng shui. If any of the fish die, don't waste time mourning your loss. The dead fish will have absorbed the misfortune meant for a resident of the house, and no harm will come to you as long as the deceased is replaced immediately.

Sitting quietly, doing nothing, spring comes, and the grass grows by itself ZEN SAYING

New Organic

Much of today's gardening is about attitude. Lack of horticultural knowledge, plus the uncanny ability to kill plants as soon as look at them, has convinced many people that green fingers will never be theirs. But you can still transform your outside space, especially if you use Eastern-style planting techniques. For starters, clear out all your clutter and replace the ubiquitous geranium-in-a-pot with the swaying grace of hardy ornamental grasses. These suit all soils and locations, look good for most of the year round, and are satisfyingly quivery, even in the lightest of winds.

Golden or black bamboo is another excellent choice for Oriental gardens. Easy to care for, not to mention the world's fastest growing plant, sometimes increasing in height by over 1 m (3 ft) a day, bamboo introduces subtle movement as well as height. The feathery foliage of silver and grey-leaved plants also look good in Eastern-style gardens, providing an interesting textural contrast to linear decking and softly rounded pebbles, while a graphic look is easily attained by filling textured planters with spiky succulents and fashionable Miscanthus grasses.

Left **Hardy ornamental grasses, fast-growing bamboo and easy-to-care for gravel are simple ways to create a low-maintenance garden with a contemporary Eastern spin.**
Right **The famous Zen garden of Tofukuji, in Kyoto, Japan.**

Zen Gardens

The Zen garden is ideal for those who want to enjoy their outside space but can't be bothered to grow anything. Concentrating on horticultural features rather than flowers, the meticulous arrangement of stones, shrubs, water, trees and sand has evolved into an art form, where a perfect balance of yin and yang allows the life-giving forces of nature to reach their full potential.

The ideal Zen garden revolves around three main features. The first is the 'tsukabi' or water basin, a simple, rounded stone with a recess or dip filled with water. Beside the stone there is a ladle, used to scoop the water up so that the hands and face can be washed before entering the tea house. (Zen gardens originally derived from rituals associated with drinking tea, while cleansing at the water basin stems from the belief that true and natural beauty cannot be seen if it is concealed by impurities.)

The second feature in the Zen garden is the 'ishidoro', or stone lantern. This squat, house-shaped lamp is symbolic of a guiding light, steering one safely along life's treacherous path, and is often raised on a plinth. (It is also a practical object, preventing gardeners from stumbling into the water feature when night falls and the sake bottle is no longer full!)

The third component is stepping stones – usually created from large, rounded boulders – placed to aesthetic advantage to work with the garden's natural shape or, from a practical point of view, to forge a pathway across a soggy lawn. Those who desire plants should choose rounded ones for good feng shui (roundness mimics the shape of a coin and symbolizes wealth and prosperity). Traditional Zen gardens also contain a tea house, a moon-viewing pavilion and stone or wooden seats for quiet contemplation.

Opposite **Decking provides the perfect platform for summer lounging. Accessorize with silk cushions, a kimono wrap and a pot of delicately scented jasmine tea.**
Left **A mini-Zen garden is a must for urban homeowners; ritualize sand-raking and pebble arrangement on a daily basis to help focus the mind.**
Below **An Oriental version of the ubiquitous Dr Scholl's.**

Get the Look

Those people who want a Zen look in their gardens, but don't want to go for the full-on treatment, can opt for a handful of effective details instead. Ideas include installing a simply structured wooden bench for meditating under; planting a native Japanese cedar tree; or making a peaceful shrine, complete with a Buddha centrepiece. Alternatively, you could divide off different 'rooms' in the garden with bamboo screens, or build a cost-effective wooden bridge. Fretwork pergolas and gazebos also add a dash of Orientalia, as do dry-stone valleys, quince bushes, weeping willows and bonsai trees.

Those of us who live in high-rise apartments or flats with tiny balconies will find installing a moon-viewing pavilion a bit of a problem – however attractive the concept – but even those with limited space can reap the benefits of Eastern horticulture. Decorate small balconies with artful pebble arrangements and pots of *helitchron* grass, and fill window boxes with aromatic herbs. Decking also works well, and looks particularly good in small backyards (the best is Bankari, an Indonesian hardwood, which becomes greyer and more beautiful over time).

Homeowners lacking in any outside space whatsoever, can get to grips with nature courtesy of a mini-Zen garden – a model of the real thing which can be raked into various calming formations to help the user concentrate his or her mind.

Petal Power

Statement-making plants are big news for anyone looking to Easternize their home. Not only do houseplants bring vibrant colour into your living space, but varieties such as jasmine, stephanotis and gardenias produce essential oils to scent, soothe and purify. In addition, watching a plant gradually reveal a flower from a bud keeps you in touch with the cycle of nature.

To evoke a sensuous exotic atmosphere, fashionable houseplants such as palms, bamboo growing in water, *fritillaria* with its pointy flowers, or a tray of wheatgrass offer the perfect choice. Sculptural spikes, such as aloe vera plants (the current favourite in Western homes, in spite of bad feng shui associations), contrast with traditional Eastern bonsai trees, while orchids earn their expensive price tag, thanks to a rare ability to absorb carbon monoxide at night and release oxygen during the day. (They also flower for six to eight weeks, brightening Western interiors during the winter months and, if cared for properly, will flower year after year.)

Flowering plants with sturdy roots or bulbs do not have to sit in earth to survive;

an alternative way to pot them is by placing them in an attractive glass container – a storm lantern, vase or tumbler will do – together with smooth pebbles collected from the beach. Simply build up the pebbles in your container, then carefully bed plants. Place more pebbles around the plants to hold them in position and water sparingly, just below the bulbs or roots.

As well as imbuing your space with a feeling of light and growth, large houseplants like ferns or palm trees can also be used as room dividers, creating the Eastern-style room-within-a-room look. In addition, plants add to the humidity of a room, not only through the water you pour onto them, but also via their leaves. In fact, anything leafy is bound to be medicinal, purifying the air by drawing in carbon dioxide and replenishing it with oxygen. Not only that, but recent research shows that certain houseplants can also filter the domestic pollutants released from cigarette smoke and chemical cleaners – with rubber plants earning top marks for their remarkable ability to reduce environmental toxins.

Above **Orchids flower for six to eight weeks, brightening Western interiors during the long winter months.**
Above left and right **The fastest-growing plant in the world, bamboo is capable of increasing in height by more than 1 m (3 ft) a day.**

Details

Even the smallest horticultural elements can help to 'naturalize' your home. Plates in the shape of leaves, chrysanthemum heads floating in a shallow bowl of water, tropical leaves used as placemats and floral wallpaper with an Oriental spin all lend organic exotica, as does a single flower stem or branch of blossom enclosed in a white porcelain sake bottle.

Alternatively, you could take a leaf out of fashion designer Koji Tatsuno's book and line your drapes with rose petals, or buy some flower garland curtains – plastic petals simply strung onto white twine and suspended from bamboo poles. Black-and-white framed flower prints are also effective, as are the new rash of table lights depicting leaves, flowers or feathers illuminated behind a Perspex screen.

Opposite **Fashion designer Koji Tatsuno inserted real rose petals into the floaty drapes of his bedroom window.**
Above **Floral-garland curtains manage to be both pretty and kitsch.**
Left **Inspiration from the world of nature provides organic silhouettes for a range of Perspex table lamps modelled on professional light boxes.**

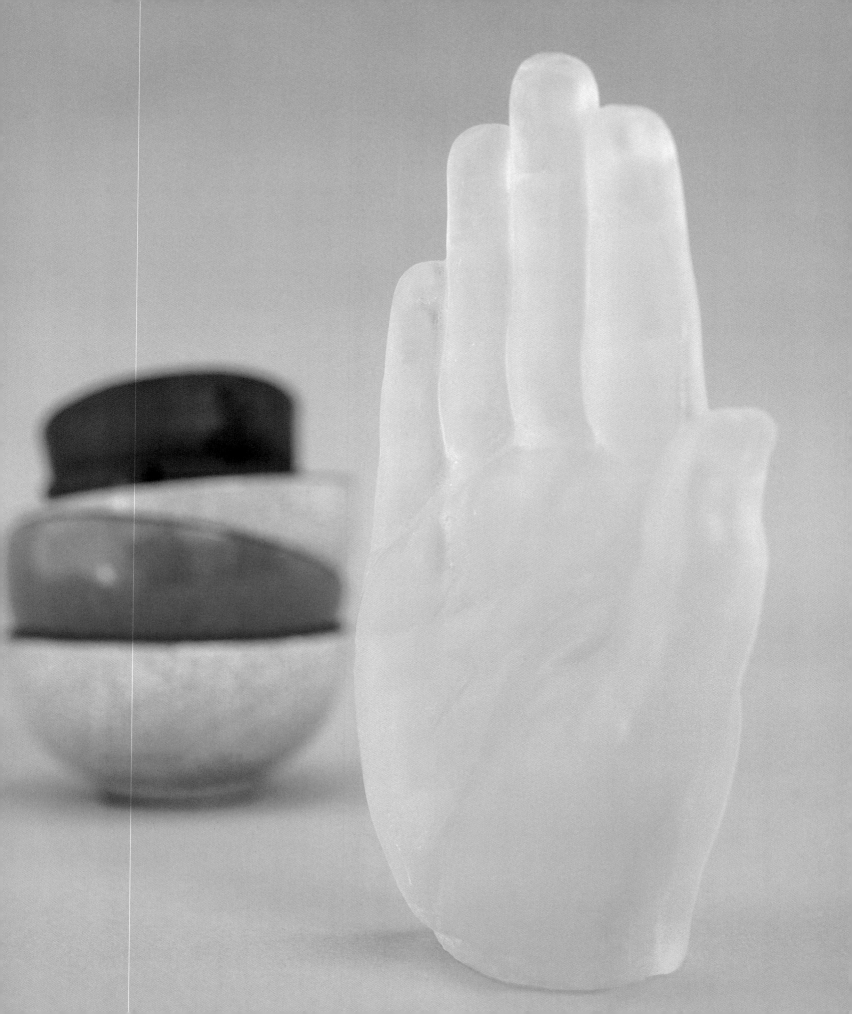

4 Enlightenment is like the moon reflected on the water ... The whole moon and the entire sky are reflected in one dewdrop on the grass DOGEN

Never has spirituality been as important as it is in the dawn of the new millennium. Thanks to a combination of technological advances, round-the-clock shopping and the cult of the celebrity, our souls have become starved of spiritual sustenance, resulting in a quest for rejuvenation which has led us back to the home. Turning our living spaces into mini-temples, where we can reflect on the important things in life, is the contemporary alternative to going to church, and while our desire to re-connect with the environment is reflected in organic furniture and natural furnishings, our accessories illustrate the need to create a spiritual haven, full of happy vibes, good smells and soothing sounds.

Eschewing Occidental spiritualism for Oriental practices, Westerners are turning to the ancient religions and philosophies of the East: Buddhism is attracting wave upon wave of Western converts, while these days, calling in the feng shui expert scarcely raises an eyebrow. Shrines depicting Buddhas

Living in Harmony

or Hindu gods are as prevalent as those featuring Western religious icons, although the essence of the new spirituality lies not so much in religious belief as sensory perception. What we want is a soothing place in which to escape from the stresses and strains of daily life.

Following the administrations of the feng shui expert – who corrects the position of our beds, re-hangs our mirrors and moves our workstations in order to harness the maximum flow of chi – we are then free to furnish our homes with sensory accessories such as wind chimes (to soothe the soul), candles (to re-create the timelessness of ancient cathedrals), and incense (to calm the nerves). Minimalism also has its place in the spiritual home. Simple ornaments which balance yin and yang create a soothing focus for meditation and help to counteract the visual chaos of neon lights, garish advertising hoardings and supermarket shelves loaded with a plethora of perplexing choices. By the same token, the intrinsic qualities of time-honoured arts and crafts, such as asymmetrical calligraphy and decorative wood carving, also help to restore equilibrium.

Creating a harmonious living space is integral to life in the Far East and the more Oriental practices we adopt – such as infusing our homes with calming aromas and creating a quite corner for daily contemplation – the greater our spiritual awareness. With this in mind, the next four sections feature the best ways to create a serene living environment. The basics of feng shui are covered in Free the Spirit, while Natural High looks at the benefits of aromatherapy, crystal gazing and the modern-day shrine. The key to successful ornament arrangement is covered in Yin and Yang, while Art House stresses the timeless beauty of Eastern art – from the purity of Japanese porcelain to Vietnamese block painting and the contemporary fashion for utilitarian craftware.

Natural High

Feng Shui Made Easy

The art of feng shui derives from the Chinese Taoist science for divining the healthy and prosperous layout of the home (in addition to its relationship with other buildings). Practised for the past 4,000 years, feng shui is about harnessing chi (the vital life force) and avoiding sha (noxious vapours). To achieve this, a combination of science, intuition, astrology, mysticism and geometry is applied, together with basic common sense.

Over the past few years feng shui has become increasingly popular with Westerners. Countless books have been published on the subject, while an increasing number of homeowners (as opposed to big businesses, which were the first to jump on the bandwagon) are consulting feng

shui experts for advice on the layout of their homes. Feng shui has even affected the housing market, with nervous housebuyers calling in a practitioner to find out if their prospective purchase has the necessary flow of chi.

Understandably, this is proving to be a thorn in the sides of estate agents, many of whom are beginning to fear the new army of consultants and the influence they wield. While fewer than five per cent of housebuyers bother to invest in a full structural survey, a growing number are spending £400-plus on feng shui experts, with some clients pulling out of sales at the last minute. However, choosing not to buy a house simply because the hedge or

wall that it looks onto may block energy is perhaps taking things a little bit too far.

Feng shui is a science, but its most realistic component is common sense, combined with an aesthetic sense of balance. If you live in a cluttered environment, you are more than likely to be less productive than if you live in a calmer, more organized one. Similarly, light interiors harness more energy than darker ones, while plants, water and organic colours appeal to our basic instinct to connect with the environment. Achieving a synergy of function and aesthetics goes a long way towards reducing the stress induced by bad planning, and is far more likely to protect you from bad vibes than if your home

overlooks a spiky church spire – symbolic of a dagger, and horribly inauspicious according to Chinese thinking.

'Feng shui is about decorating with a sixth sense,' says Eddie Wong, a London-based practitioner, and advocate for making simple changes to harness maximum energy in the home. 'If the rooms you live in have good feng shui you will sleep better, live better and accomplish more,' he says. And while many of the feng shui pointers published in books and magazines are valid, some of them are plain ridiculous: 'You hear about where to put the toilet and closing the lid, but that's all crap,' continues Wong. 'If you find your best energy, you get the best of everything.'

Below **In tandem with the fashion for loft apartments comes the desire to have your living space feng shuied by a legitimate practitioner. Alternatively, you can do it yourself by adhering to a few simple guidelines and following your instincts.**

Far left **Quartz crystals are viewed by the Chinese as the aspirins of feng shui – good for curing just about everything.**
Left **Fresh flowers bring energy into the home, but they also have a detrimental effect once they start to wither.**

Helpful Pointers for Good Feng Shui

According to experts, feng shui masters aim to correct whatever is causing energy – and therefore good luck – to stagnate, leak, flow uncontrollably or become convoluted. Below, are a few pointers to help harness maximum chi:

- Large mirrors are excellent for enhancing the stale energy of a cramped space and are especially recommended for tiny halls. Place a mirror on a wall that does not face the door as this will cause all the good fortune to dissipate.

- Quartz crystals are considered the aspirins of feng shui – good for curing almost anything. Hang them wherever energy may escape – at the end of a corridor, for example, and place them on sharp corners to dissolve bad chi.

- Water (such as an aquarium) in the room where you sleep causes you to lose money.

- Plants and trees in the home are auspicious because the wood element signifies growth and development.

- At least once a week open two windows in two different rooms to let fresh air sweep away any stale yin air. Try to do this on a sunny day to bring in vibrant yang energy, which attracts good fortune.

- While fresh flowers bring yang energy into living spaces, they can also become depressingly yin once they wither and die. Replace dying flowers with a fresh bunch the moment they start to fade.

Top left **Tall stems help to bring wood into interiors.** Bottom left **Candles introduce fire into the home – one of five elements thought to maximize harmony and balance.**

The Five Elements

For maximum harmony and balance in the home, Orientals believe that each of the five elements – water, fire, wood, earth and metal – be represented. Listed below are some ideas on how to introduce them into your living space:

- **Water**
  Object enhancement aquamarines, fountains, glass, ponds
  Colours black, blues
  Shapes curvy lines
- **Fire**
  Object enhancement lights, candles, fireplaces
  Colours reds
  Shapes pointed, triangles, zigzags
- **Wood**
  Object enhancement indoor plants, flowers, wooden objects
  Colours greens
  Shapes rectangular and tall
- **Earth**
  Object enhancement stone, crystal, rocks, pebbles, terracotta clay pots
  Colours yellows
  Shape low, wide, flat-topped items
- **Metal**
  Object enhancement electrical equipment and stainless steel, metal objects
  Colours silver, white
  Shapes round, domed, spherical

Right **The furnishings in this loft-style apartment have been arranged according to the philosophy of feng shui for ultimate calm and contentment.**

Feng Shui in the Home Office

With increasing numbers of people working from home, productive output is of prime importance. Make your home office one-hundred per cent effective with a few tips from the experts:

- The most auspicious desks are higher than standard Western styles, so place a platform underneath your workstation.
- The door into your office should open onto a bright, spacious and well-lit area.
- Sit facing the door and keep seating against a wall to provide support and stability.
- Avoid jagged, sharp edges by ensuring there are no corners intersecting your desk or chair, and that nothing sharp is pointing at you. (This rules out cacti and yucca plants.)
- Company logos and stationery should be clear and simple. Resist encasing any portion of a logo in a circle, or you will create obstacles by imprisoning your name.
- Harmonious images, such as birds, planes or anything going up, will harness good vibes. Images of successful people, bright flowers, trees and modern cityscapes are also recommended. Avoid sunsets, waterfalls or anything with a downward motion.

Feng Shui Verging on the Absurd

- Advisors are being called in to re-design the layout of some major British supermarkets. The powers that be are keen to make their fruit and vegetables 'happy', moving tomatoes away from red peppers, and cancelling out the 'negative waves' emanating from lettuces by placing them next to 'positive' oranges.
- At trend-setting myhotel in Bloomsbury, London, the WCs are not signposted for fear that chi will read the directions, meander in and be flushed away.

Above **Burning incense stimulates the senses.**
Right **Adhering to a few basic feng shui pointers could significantly increase productivity in the workplace.**

Free the Spirit

All evidence of truth comes only from the senses NIETZSCHE

Left Creating a personal shrine fulfils the need for quiet contemplation on a daily basis.
Below Joss sticks have been renamed Aroma Stix for 'style-conscious' modern hippies.

One of the most important aspects of life in the Far East is the veneration of the spirit world. From regular grave-sweeping in China (which is supposed to appease the souls of the deceased and prevent them from returning to wreak hell on earth) to daily offerings of food, nurturing the blessed departed is a time-consuming business.

In Thailand, the sheer variety of 'phi' (spirits) outnumbers the population many times over. Almost every dwelling place features a spirit house, generally set on top of a post, and located on a site selected following complex astrological considerations. In domestic residences the spirit house may resemble a Thai dwelling, while hotels and offices tend to favour elaborate mini-temples. Both serve as an abode for locality spirits, and are dutifully maintained with daily offerings of food, flowers and incense.

The Balinese are also hot on religious observance. Not counting the shrines in every home, there are supposedly 20,000 temples on the island honouring numerous Hindu gods believed to possess the power to bestow fear or favour on ordinary mortals. As a result, baskets of plaited palms are laden with fruit and flowers in a bid to appease the demons and honour the gods.

Shrines

Thanks to our continued fascination with all things Eastern, shrines are becoming an increasingly popular feature in Western homes. As our lives become more hectic, so too does our desire to seek meaning from age-old rituals, such as spiritual observance. The presence of a shrine fulfils the basic human need to retreat to a quiet corner in order to meditate upon the things we love, and focus on our dreams and aspirations.

It doesn't matter what you include as part of your shrine as long as it has meaning for you. Simply select an uncluttered part of the room, lay down a cushion or mat on which to sit and meditate, and arrange a few of your favourite things (a jade necklace, piece of quartz, shells or driftwood) on a table or chest. As a central feature, choose a pertinent image or object on which to focus your concentration (it could be a bronze Buddha, a Christian icon, a photograph of a loved one – even a flowerhead floating in a bowl of water), and surround it with candles and incense.

Eastern Fragrances

Scenting the air has always been a predominant feature in Eastern life. In ancient Japan, scent-clocks, which released a different incense every hour, were used to tell the time: for example, you might have awoken to fresh citrusy smells and gone to sleep in an atmosphere infused with somnolent spices.

Today, the Chinese continue to light joss sticks as well as place perfume burners by every front door. They also used to keep pieces of aromatic tree bark tucked in the laundry. At one point, even Chinese money was scented. For most of us, however, the idea of scenting a space, rather than just our bodies is a recent phenomenon.

Whether you burn joss sticks (below)**, an incense coil** (opposite) **or scented cones** (right)**, watching lazy spirals of smoke is calming and meditative.**

The revival of scenting the home, after almost 200 fragrance-free years, is partly due to the huge success of aromatherapy over the past few years. In Japan, Dr Shizuo Torii has demonstrated the stimulating or sedative effects of various essential oils on the brain, and some Japanese companies are now using 'aroma systems' in their buildings, pumping soothing oils like lavender and rose into reception areas and lemon (shown to reduce keyboard errors) into computer sites.

The longing to be pure and natural, so well established in the cosmetics industry, is spilling into our attitude towards the home. These days the desire to scent the atmosphere with fragrant aromas, rather than chemicals, has led to the marketing of products such as Aveda's angelic smelling Dish Cleaner and L'Occitane's Linen Lavender Water – helping to lift the tedium of household chores.

In addition, hip hotels such as the Paramount and Royalton in New York have both caught on to the whiff of sensory success, spraying their bedrooms with Fresh Air Supergreen Fine Linen Spray by Mio. By the same token, cutting-edge stores such as Muji and Habitat have also launched aromatic room sprays.

Incense

Known to enhance feelings of well-being as well as stimulating the senses, incense is still the mainstay of religious observances in the Far East, often overriding the primary importance of prayer. A case in point is Vietnam, where visits to pagodas are informal, social affairs. People come and go, chat to monks, drink tea and present offerings. But no one ever returns from a temple trip without burning incense.

Nor is lighting a joss stick simply a matter of striking a match. On festival days, the Vietnamese must burn an entire packet of incense sticks, or a smaller number depending on the occasion, just so long as the number used is an odd one. Burn an even number of joss sticks and you are literally playing with fire. After lighting the incense, worshippers stand in contemplation before the altar for a few minutes. They then make respectful bowing movements before placing the burning sticks in a small urn filled with fragrant ash. The rising smoke symbolizes communication with the spirit world and allows worshippers to maintain contact with their ancestors – or to present wishes to one of the many Gods in the Vietnamese pantheon.

In the West, burning incense is not just an olfactory pleasure; watching the smoke curl and

Better to light one candle than to curse the darkness
UNKNOWN

Scented Candles

spiral upwards is also calming, meditative and deeply hip. Formerly associated with the 1960s and 1970s when burning incense was viewed as part of the dope-smoking culture, today's joss sticks have got their act together. Not only are they now known as Aroma Stix, but the original tatty packaging has been replaced by glossy lacquered containers.

Cedar incense spirals, originally found in Chinese temples, are also great for devotees of Eastern aromas. The perfect way to scent an entire room (they are also great insect deterrents), incense spirals can be hung inside or out, and last for hours. Additional Eastern fragrances can be wrought by mixing a cocktail of exotic scents: place a perfumed silk cushion next to a bowl of scented pebbles for instance, or fill your drawers with a mix of spicy amber sachets and tangy lime leaves.

Alternatively, you can toss a combination of frangipani petals and rose-scented pebbles into the bath to infuse the water with a heady collection of different aromas. Kelly Hoppen's new collection of fragrant feng shui home accessories (called 'Turiya', which means a state of ultimate harmony with one's inner being) is also proving popular, especially with Hollywood's more demanding divas.

Thanks to the influence of Buddhism, a sense of spirituality pervades almost every aspect of Thai life. Numerous festivals and feasts are held throughout the year, with incense and candles smouldering throughout. One of the most beautiful of Thai festivals, Loy Krathong, centres on the floating of small candles and incense down-river. Placed inside small cups made out of banana leaves, the 'krathongs' are taken to the banks of waterways when the full moon rises, and the candles and incense lit. A prayer is said as the glowing vessels are launched into the water.

For thousands of years candles were a part of everyday life, illuminating dark nights and used in religious rituals across the world. Candlelight is the essence of spirituality, representing faith and hope in many lands and customs. Today, now that they are no longer essential, candles are seen as a luxurious way to create instant atmosphere proving as popular at rock concerts as they are at dinner parties, where intimate spaces are defined through the creation of atmospheric shadows.

In tandem with the fashion for turning your home into a peaceful retreat is the vogue for filling it with candles. Nothing can make or mark your mood more quickly than a scented candle, and there are dozens of different

varieties to choose from, including a wide range of aromatherapy candles fragranced with Eastern-inspired scents such as jasmine, orange blossom, frangipani, honeysuckle and lily of the valley. Alternatively, you can spice up the atmosphere with the natural aromas of amber, musk and cinnamon, or recall Eastern sensibilities with feng shui candles offering the essences of water, fire, metal, wood and earth in elegant wax columns. Even tea-scented candles are now available, with lapsang souchong the number-one favourite.

Herb-encrusted candles are also becoming popular, while a galaxy of tiny tea-lights slotted into sleek, lacquered containers help to conjure up Eastern nights in a flash. Candles floating in water and larger candles with four or five wicks apiece create a spiritual feel, as do elegant tapers in beeswax. Light a handful and push them into a bowl of sand for a religious feel, but remember to light candles using tapers: hands-on spirituality does not include painful, burnt fingers.

Even furniture designers are lighting up. Take your cue from Matthew Hilton, whose candles come in bone-china holders so that as the wax burns down messages such as 'light-hearted' and 'light of my life' appear in the china.

Jade

Venerated for its beauty as well as its magical powers, jade is viewed by the Chinese as the most precious of stones. According to myth, when the god Pan Gu died, his breath became the wind and clouds, his muscles soil, and the marrow of his bones jade and pearls. As a result, the Chinese have long-since buried their dead with jade discs called 'li', in order to ensure harmony between heaven and earth.

To this day, many Chinese wear a similar disc around their necks in the hope that it will bring them good luck as well as offer protection from evil spirits. Jade is also said to be an accurate representation of health: if the disc glows, then the vitality of the wearer is assured, but if he or she falls ill, the disc will become tarnished.

Coolly tactile, there are two types of jade – 'nephrite' in varying shades of green and 'jadeite' which comes in many colours including white, brown and red. As far as home furnishings are concerned, jade ornaments in the shape of Buddhas, dragons and tigers are as attractive as they are auspicious.

Crystals, Dreamcatchers, Wind Chimes and Moonbells

Frequently viewed as the exclusive domain of new-agers, the healing powers of crystals have long been undermined. In the spiritual enlightenment of the new millennium, however, even hardened sceptics are hanging lumps of rose quartz in their windows in order to energize their space by filling it with rainbow-coloured prisms of moving light.

Decorating your windows with a feather dreamcatcher is another way to maximize the spiritual potential of your home. Crafted like a spider's web and adorned with feathers, beads and crystals, dreamcatchers are said to ensnare good dreams in their net, allowing the dreamer to carry them through life. Also said to draw good things to a person, dream-catchers represent the elements of earth, water, fire and air, with each one addressing different areas: air expands and uplifts your mood; water represents intuition and healing powers; earth symbolizes wisdom, and fire is radiant and purifying.

In China and Japan the importance of sound – both inside and out – has long been emphasized. And while the Japanese have always ensured that the tinkle of water and moon bells is within hearing distance, the Chinese are committed fans of wind chimes, swearing that the mellifluous jangling helps to slow down the pace of fast-flowing chi. For best results, hang one in a long, narrow space such as a passage or hallway to prevent energy speeding out of control.

Yin and Yang

Look for the good in everything so that you absorb the quality of beauty

PARAMAHANSA YOGANANDA, SPIRITUAL GURU

What is Yin and Yang?

Because the energies of your personal space are in a constant state of flux, finding the perfect balance between the opposing forces of yin and yang are essential for creating a calming, cosmic atmosphere. Yin is cool, dark and lifeless, while yang is hot and bright and full of life. According to ancient Eastern philosophies, if you strike the perfect chord between these two, you will enjoy good luck. (A quick and easy way to achieve this is by creating a comfortable balance between light and shade, adding slightly more light in order to enhance yang energy.)

Left and right **Balance yin and yang through the aesthetic art of ornament arrangement.**

The Art of Ornament Arrangement

In the Far East the art of arranging ornaments requires discipline and control. Ideally, you want to display single objects, or a collection of pieces with a linking feature, such as shape, texture or colour. The aim is to emphasize the intrinsic beauty of every piece, as this method has a far greater impact than displaying a clutter of disparate objects, however beautiful each piece may be individually.

The maxim to live simply, consider shapes and furnish with objects and materials that reflect light or cast beautiful shadows is

particularly evident in Japanese homes. Often
seen as overly spare in their furnishing aesthetic,
the average Japanese likes ornaments as much
as the next man, but he also stays true to the
harmonious marriage of form and function –
or yin and yang. In his view, a single, beautiful
piece which calms and concentrates the mind –
as well as being useful – is infinitely superior
to a collection of less precious ones, while the
process of possession-pruning helps him to
appreciate objects with true value and style.

Quality, not quantity, is the main concern
in the art of Eastern ornament arrangement.
The Japanese choose pure shapes and straight
lines, preferring simplicity to intricacy, and (as
in a hand-thrown potter's bowl), organic shapes
to manufactured perfection. Balance is also
important, although designs do not have to be
regimental. Uneven numbers create interest,
while varying the height of objects is also
visually effective. A good example is to
juxtapose a couple of tall vases with a few
mid-height jars and a cup and saucer, in order
to draw the eye inwards and upwards through
the group and create an impression of depth.

Achieving a harmonious balance of yin and
yang requires a good eye as well as a natural
instinct for what looks – and feels – right. The
art of ornament arrangement cannot be taught.
It relies, instead, on the impact caused by a
group of objects that work together, in addition
to the blending of harmonious colours and
shapes that relate well to the space around
them. As a result, there are no hard and fast
rules as to what decorative objects you can –
and cannot – display. Trial and error is the
best method – as well as following a few
simple guidelines as to what works best.

Yin and Yang

Choosing Objects

Displaying similar items, which perhaps differ in texture or size, is a simple starting point for successful arrangements. A collection of three baskets, ranging from large to small, is both decorative and accessible, and this discipline can also be employed with objects such as vases, bowls, teacups or framed prints. From here, you can progress to more advanced configurations, fusing natural pieces with spiritual ones, such as a bowl of oranges with a silver candlestick, and literary pieces with antique ones, such as a stack of hardbacks with an antique Chinese figurine.

Displaying memorabilia with ephemera – try a collection of black-and-white postcards with a couple of old coins – is another good contrast, while the value of found and natural objects cannot be over-emphasized. Driftwood, quails' eggs and starfish are all attractive, while shells and pebbles remain the favourite choice because, whether they are displayed singly or thrown together in a stone bowl or glass trough, they always look great. Similarly, everyday objects like flowers and fruit often make the most effective still lifes, thanks to their intrinsic beauty.

Contrast and Texture

Some of the most interesting juxtapositions come from playing shapes off against one another. Soft, fluid pieces such as a circular fruit bowl on a square table, or a squat Japanese lantern on top of a Chinese wedding chest are the perfect complement to hard surfaces. Similarly, objects displayed within the natural framework of an alcove also look great, while contrasting textures, like a rough piece of driftwood with a smooth pebble, or a solid pottery bowl with a wicker-work tray, are tried and tested combinations that always work well.

Pictures

Picture hanging is another important aspect of Eastern style. If you have a big enough wall, fix one image dead centre, and leave it at that. By contrast, a collection of same-size prints by one artist can look very effective, as long as they are similarly, and simply, framed. If you choose to display pictures by different artists, try to keep within the same family of colours, and allow each image to 'breathe' by leaving enough wall space between images.

Banners, in a single colour – or with a clean graphic design – make an effective and colourful backdrop for ornamental displays, while a hessian runner – laid along the length of a shelf in a horizontal strip – provides textural contrast to collections of silky-smooth ceramics.

Ikebana

In accordance with the spare aesthetic of Zen decorating, the Japanese belief that a few well-chosen pieces are worth more than a pile of clutter is illustrated by *ikebana* – or the art of flower ornamentation. Instead of arranging a bunch of mixed flowers in a vase, a single, elegant stem, bloom, spray or branch of twisted willow is used. In the case of the latter, the contrast of the curling wood and the delicate bloom is considered to be the perfect balance of yin and yang.

We shape clay into a pot, but it is the emptiness inside that holds whatever we want TAO TE CHING

Art House

Porcelain

Eastern art has long been venerated for its purity of execution and diversity of form. Ranging from porcelain to painting, and craft to calligraphy, Western art takes its cue from the ancient influences of China, Japan, Vietnam, Thailand and Indonesia, with porcelain remaining the most famous media.

Invented by the Chinese in the seventh century AD, some of the earliest ceramics are still prized for their pure shapes today. One example is celadon, a green, glazed earthenware, dating back to 300 AD, and still made in north Vietnam using traditional techniques. Similarly, the blue-and-white porcelain styles invented during the Ming Dynasty were so popular in sixteenth-century Europe that countries such as Britain, France and Germany competed with one another in a bid to discover the secret of its manufacture. Not surprisingly the Germans won, with the first hard-paste porcelain manufactured in 1709. Traditional Chinese decorations were added later, with round-faced Chinamen in lampshade hats sitting beside winding streams, and women in patterned robes drinking tea in bamboo pavilions. Willow trees were a recurring motif, and while designs became progressively more Westernized (with transfers replacing hand-painting in the nineteenth century), the Willow Pattern, devised by Josiah Spode from an original Chinese design, has remained a ubiquitous feature in Western dining rooms to this day.

As tastes changed, moving away from the baroque styles of the seventeenth century to anti-classical rococo, collectors shifted their attention from the robust decoration of Ming porcelain to something slightly more refined. As a result, Japanese ceramics came into vogue, especially the elegant, asymmetrical designs of Kakiemon porcelain, which featured sparse patterns picked out in a palette of brick red, clear blue, pale yellow and turquoise green.

Left and far left **Chinese and Japanese figures are popular motifs on contemporary porcelain.**

Porcelain Today

Tagged as the 'art of the moment', modern ceramics concentrate on fluid lines, simple shapes and delicately coloured and textured glazes. Taking their cue from the Eastern ideal of purity, proportion and function (rather than pattern), contemporary ceramics couldn't be plainer. Simple white dinner sets top wedding lists across Britain and the USA, followed by minimalist bands of colour, also on white (for the adventurous). Japanese porcelain is also popular, thanks to its earthy asymmetry and sparsity of design. Polka dots are currently leading the field, with Japanese calligraphy painted onto a muddy palette of greens and browns bringing up the rear.

Craft

Best known for the beauty of their silverware, the Thais are also experts in decorative woodcarving, adorning teak furniture with traditional motifs such as lotus flowers, serpents and dragons 'borrowed' from China. Vietnam also has a long history of craftsmanship – including lacquerware and woodcuts – the best examples of which come from the Tranh Lang Ho village paintings. Known as Ho painting, the art of woodcutting existed from as early as the eleventh century when, in accordance with tradition, whole villages were given over to the art of block painting.

Today, craftsmen still use natural colours – as well as making their own paper – preparing the blocks in classic designs, which include good luck symbols, historical figures, popular allegories and social commentary. Good fortune is symbolized by a fat pig decorated with garlands, while a hen surrounded by chicks signals prosperity, and a rooster peace and courage.

Back in the West, utilitarian Eastern craftware is currently being hailed as the new folk art. Freshly imported from farms and fields across China, Vietnam and Thailand, brightly painted wooden 'bells' (more commonly seen hanging around the necks of buffalo), rice baskets, earthenware jars and woven containers are being snapped up by homeowners keen to cash in on rural chic. Even Alessi, famous for their hi-tech designs, have gone green, with a collection of straw bowls covered in beeswax.

Far left **Take your cue from the world's best-dressed tables and opt for porcelain in simple shapes and muted colours.** Left **A simple calligraphy pattern lifts this duvet cover out of the ordinary.**

Calligraphy and Art

Described by a Western art historian as 'ciphers of transcendence', calligraphy is viewed by the Japanese and Chinese as the highest form of artistic expression. From its earliest beginnings, Zen found a natural affinity with the spontaneous quality of calligraphy (the first stroke is the final stroke – there can be no subsequent correction), while to this day, writing in China has maintained its single standard and style, despite the numerous spoken dialects. In Vietnam, calligraphy has been replaced by the Roman alphabet (which was introduced by foreign missionaries) and is now only used by scholars. In the West, the graphic beauty of calligraphy has captured our collective imaginations. Hanging from scrolls or framed under glass, calligraphy also adorns furnishings – from glass tumblers to upholstery, and cotton duvet covers to candle holders.

There has always been a close connection between Chinese painting and calligraphy. Ancient Chinese words started as pictograms, and while each has developed in a separate direction, there remain inextricable ties between the two. As a rule, classical Chinese painters have extensive training in calligraphy, while calligraphers have experience in painting. Both forms are often present together in one piece of work, created with the same writing and painting utensils. These are referred to in China as the 'Four Treasures of Study', including a bamboo brush, ink, rubbing stone and paper. In addition, both calligraphy and painting are considered scholarly pursuits in China, although calligraphy has always been

藝子
みさえ
吉田屋
中居
とき

長喜画

held in higher regard. Literati painters, for example, judged works by their combination of painting, poetry and calligraphy; success in all three deemed paintings as high art.

Classical Chinese paintings can be grouped into six categories: landscape, portraits, flowers, birds, bamboo and stone, animals and palaces and other buildings – with landscape the most favoured form. Called 'Mountain Water Paintings' in Chinese, subject matter included, not surprisingly, mountains and water, accented with clouds, mist and trees. Human figures feature only as tiny specks, reflecting the Chinese philosophy on the relationship between individuals and the outside world, where human beings are seen as subservient to their surroundings.

Japanese wood-block prints have been available to Westerners for over 100 years. They are instantly recognizable, thanks to a handful of popular images such as Katsushika

Above **Origami squares make a contemporary Eastern collage.**
Opposite **The appeal of Japanese art lies in its strong lines and flat blocks of colour.**
Left **Aesthetic to the last, Japanese packaging elevates everyday items into objects of beauty.**

Hokusai's *Great Wave off Kanagawa*. The composition, colours and content of Japanese prints inspired works by Vincent Van Gogh, Edouard Manet and James McNeill Whistler, among others. Modern Japanese art includes graphic wall banners which feature simple stark patterns in circles and squares.

Shanghai Girlie Posters

The fashion for 'Shanghai Girlie posters' is fast gaining momentum, with collectors exhibiting their artworks to growing public interest. Occasionally more politely referred to by their Chinese name of 'yuefenpai', or calendar posters, these beguiling relics of pre-war advertising began as New Year gifts from Western firms to Chinese clients. They later flowered into a distinct art form, appearing as wall-hangings in Chinese homes throughout the 1920s and 1930s.

The posters show exquisite Chinese beauties with unblemished complexions – some of them nightclub stars, one of them a well-known transvestite – holding cigarettes, straddling motorbikes or extolling the virtues of batteries, soap or cosmetics. Some are very risqué, while many of the models adopt poses copied from Hollywood movie stars such as Marlene Dietrich and Mae West. Together with the painterly quality of the posters, the fey Chinese backdrops featuring porcelain vases, sprigs of plum blossom and cute Pekinese dogs is a kitsch-lover's delight – while the concept of canines as must-have accessories is clearly not a new one.

Resources

Bathrooms

Alternative Plans
9 Hester Road
London SW11 4AN
Tel: 020 7228 6460
www.alternative-plans.co.uk

Original Bathrooms
143–5 Kew Road
Richmond, Surrey TW9 2PN
Tel: 020 8940 7554

William Garvey
Tel: 01404 841430
(Wooden sinks and baths)

Decking

Archadeck
The Old Shipyard
Gainsborough
Lincolnshire DN21 1NG
Tel: 01977 704963
www.archadeck.co.uk

The London Decking Company
Unit 6, St Saviour's Wharf
Mill Street
London SE1 2BE
Tel: 020 7231 3735
www.londondecking.co.uk

Redwood Decking and Landscaping
Bridge Inn Nurseries
Moss Side, Formby
Merseyside L37 0AF
Tel: 01704 832355

Flooring

Amtico
42 Kingfield Road
Coventry CV6 5AA
Tel: 0800 667766 for stockists
www.amtico.co
(Swimming pool tiles)

Attica
543 Battersea Park Road
London SW11 3BL
Tel: 020 7738 1234
(Bronze and pewter ceramic tiles)

Blanc de Bierges
Eastrea Road
Whittlesey
Peterborough
Cambridge PE7 2AG
Tel: 01733 202566
www.blancdebierges.com
(Concrete pavers)

Granite & Marble International
Pensbury Place, Wandsworth Road
London SW8 4TR
Tel: 020 7498 2742
www.stonework.co.uk

Harvey Maria
The Trident Business Centre
89 Bickersteth Road
London SW17 9SH
Tel: 020 8516 7788
www.harveymaria.co.uk
(Pebble-patterned floor tiles)

The Natural Wood Floor Company
20 Smugglers Way
London SW18 1EQ
Tel: 020 8871 9771
www.naturalwoodfloor.co.uk

The Photo Tile Company
Tel: 020 8877 3733 for stockists

Stone Age
19 Filmer Road
London SW6 7BU
Tel: 020 7385 7954
www.stone-age.co.uk

Taylor Maxwell
Taylor Maxwell House
The Promenade
Clifton
Bristol BS8 3NW
Tel: 01179 737888
(Sandstone, limestone, slate and marble)

Helene Verin
Tel: 001 212 691 1185
(Wood-effect rugs)

Furniture, Furnishings & Accessories

Alma Home
Unit D, 12–14 Greatorex Street
London E1 5NF
Tel: 020 7377 0762
www.almahome.co.uk

Altfield, Unit 2–22
Chelsea Harbour Design Centre
London SW10 0XE
Tel: 020 7351 5893
www.altfield.com

Andrew Martin International
200 Walton Street
London SW3 2JL
Tel: 020 7225 5100

Auro Organic Paint
Tel: 01799 584888 (Mail order)

Beagle Gallery
303 Westbourne Grove
London W11 2QA
Tel: 020 7229 9524

Browns Living
23–7 South Molton Street
London W1Y 1DA
Tel: 020 7491 7833
www.brownsfashion.com

Calvin Klein Home
Tel: 001 212 719 2600

Carden Cunietti
83 Westbourne Park Road
London W2 5QH
Tel: 020 7229 8559
www.carden-cunietti.com

David Champion
199 Westbourne Grove
London W11 2SB
Tel: 020 7727 6016

Channels
3 New King's Road
London SW6 4SB
www.channelsdesign.com
Tel: 020 7371 0301

Christopher Farr
212 Westbourne Grove
London W11 2RH
Tel: 020 7792 5761
www.cfarr.co.uk

Contemporary Ceramics
7 Marshall Street
London W1V 1LP
Tel: 020 7437 7605

County & Eastern
8 Redwell Street
Norwich, NR2 4FN
Tel: 01603 623107
and 3 Holland Street
London W8 4NA
Tel: 020 7938 2711

David Wainwright
251 Portobello Road
London W11 1LT
Tel 020 7792 1988
and 63 Portobello Road
London W11 3DB
Tel: 020 7727 0707

Eastern Trading Alliance
Townmead Business Centre
William Morris Way
London SW6 2SZ
Tel: 020 7731 3262 (Mail order)
www.etaco.co.uk

EFDC
18–24 Westbourne Grove
London W2 1RH
Tel: 020 7243 0203 and
94 Tottenham Court Road
London W1P 9HE
Tel: 020 7813 2092

The Futon Company
100 Battersea Rise
London SW11 1EJ
Tel: 020 7978 4498
www.thefutoncompany.co.uk

General Trading Company
144 Sloane Street
London SW1X 9BL
Tel: 020 7730 0411
www.gtc@btinternet.com

Gong
182 Portobello Road
London W11 2EB
Tel: 020 7565 4162
joplismy@hotmail.com

Gucci
33 Old Bond Street
London W1X 4HH
Tel: 020 7629 2716
www.gucci.com

Guinevere
578 King's Road
London SW6 2DY
Tel: 020 7736 2917
www.guinevere.co.uk

Habitat
Tel: 0845 6010740 for branches
www.habitat.co.uk

Harrods
87–135 Brompton Road
London SW1X 7XL
Tel: 020 7730 1234
www.harrods.com

The Holding Company
243–5 King's Road
London SW3 5EL
Tel: 020 7352 1600
www.theholdingcompany.co.uk

Indigo
59 Walcott Street
Bath BA1 5BN
Tel: 01225 311795

Jacqueline Edge
1 Courtnell Street
London W2 5BU
Tel: 020 7229 1172
www.i-i.net/jacquelineedge

Joss Graham Gallery
10 Eccleston Street
London SW1W 9LT
Tel: 020 7730 4370

Kara Kara
2a Pond Place
London SW3 6QT
Tel: 020 7591 0891

Katie Jones
155 Westbourne Grove
London W11 2SB
Tel: 020 7243 5600

Kitschen Sync
7 Earlham Street
London WC2H 9LL
Tel: 020 7497 5129
0906 6800036 (Mail order)
www.kitschensync.com

Liberty
32 Kingly Street
London W1R 5LA
Tel: 020 7734 1234
www.liberty-of-london.com

Lombok
4 Heathmans Road
London SW6 4TJ
Tel: 020 7736 5171
www.lombok.co.uk

Matahari
147 Battersea Business Centre
99–109 Lavender Hill
London SW11 5QF
Tel: 020 7228 3405

Mei Lin Oriental Antiques
5 High Street
Oxshott
Surrey KT22 0JP
Tel: 01372 843338

Minh Mang
182 Battersea Park Road
London SW11 4ND
Tel: 020 7498 3233

mint
70 Wigmore Street
London W1H 9DL
Tel: 020 7224 4406

Mufti
789 Fulham Road
London SW6 5HD
Tel: 020 7610 9123
www.mufti.co.uk

Muji
Tel: 020 7323 2208 for branches

Neal Street East
5–7 Neal Street
London WC2H 9PU
Tel: 020 7240 0135

The Neon Circus
Tel: 020 8964 3381 for enquiries

Nine Schools at Selfridges
400 Oxford Street
London W1A 1AB
Tel: 020 7629 1234
www.selfridges.com

Hikaru Noguchi
Unit 2L
Cockpit Workshops
Cockpit Yard
London WC1N 2NP
Tel: 020 7813 0883

Nom
150 Walton Street
London SW3 2JJ
Tel: 020 7584 4158

Ocean
Tel: 0870 2426283 (Mail order)
www.oceancatalogue.com

Opium
414 King's Road
London SW10 0LJ
Tel: 020 7795 0700

Orientique
40 Oak End Way
Gerrards Cross
Buckinghamshire
SL9 8BR
Tel: 01753 888361

Ornamenta
3–12 Chelsea Harbour Design Centre
Chelsea Harbour
London SW10 0XE
Tel: 020 7352 1824
www.ornamenta.co.uk

Ou Baholyodhin Studio
1st Floor
12 Greatorex Street
London E1 5NF
Tel: 020 7426 0666
www.ou-b.com

Paint and Paper Library
5 Elystan Street
London SW3 3NT
Tel: 020 7823 7755
www.paintlibrary.co.uk

Paint Magic
48 Goldbourne Road
London W10 5PR
Tel: 020 8960 9910
www.paint-magic.com

Port of Call
122 Ebury Street
London SW1 9QQ
Tel: 020 7589 4836

Emily Readett Bayley
Tel: 01400 281563 (Mail order)
www.webuk.com

SCP
135–9 Curtain Road
London EC2A 3BX
Tel: 020 7739 1869
www.scp.co.uk

Sebastian Barbagallo Antiques
15 Pembridge Road
London W11 0PS
Tel: 020 7792 3320

Snap Dragon
247 Fulham Road
London SW3 6HY
Tel: 020 7376 8889

Talisman Trading
Tel: 01634 844722 (Mail order)

Tansu
Redbrick Mill
218 Bradford Road
Batley Carr
Batley
West Yorkshire WF17 6JF
Tel: 01924 460044
www.tansu.co.uk

Jim Thompson
Unit 1–9
Chelsea Harbour Design Centre
London SW10 0XE
Tel: 020 7351 2829

Tocca
Shop
4 Brewer Street
London W1R 3FP
Tel: 020 7437 1259

Heating

Bisque Radiators
244 Belsize Road
London NW6 4BT
Tel: 020 7328 2225

Dalsouple
PO Box 140, Bridgewater
Somerset TA5 1HT
Tel: 01278 733133

Flo Rad Heating
Unit 1, Horseshoe Business Park
Lye Lane
Ricket Wood
Hertfordshire AL2 3TA
Tel: 01923 893025
www.florad.co.uk
(Underfloor)

Index